To Cousin _____

My sister _____ in _____ Christ. I loved this devotional & thought you might enjoy it also -

Hugs from my heart to yours -

XO Carole

If anyone knows how to gain *The Power to Be: Be Still, Be Grateful, Be Strong, Be Courageous*, it is my brave and bright friend, Twila! With practical wisdom, simple-to-apply insights, and rich biblical application woven with splashes of humor, this *must-read* book will lower your stress and raise your hope and joy.

—PAM FARREL, international speaker and author of forty-five books, including *Men Are Like Waffles, Women Are Like Spaghetti*, and *7 Simple Steps for Every Woman: Success in Keeping It All Together*

In a day and time when everyone struggles to persevere, *The Power to Be* brings God's promises into reach through a simplified and strategic forty-day application. Twila Belk's power statements help carry us through the tough times of life in short and memorable fashion. I see *The Power to Be* as a daily resource for women and men who desire spiritual growth and encouragement for their families.

—LINDA GOLDFARB, author of *Loving the ME God Sees*, international speaker, certified Christian life coach, and founder of Parenting Awesome Kids (LivePowerfullyNow.org)

When life feels disturbing, difficult, or distorted, *The Power to Be* brings the stability you crave in Christ. Interwoven with riveting stories from the author's life, correlating biblical examples, and probing personal questions, this book provides you with a safe place to process life's most important questions.

—MARNIE SWEDBERG, leadership mentor, international speaker, author, and media personality (Marnie.com)

Twila Belk is not only an accomplished author, she's a woman intimately acquainted with hardship. With honesty and humility, she shares insights learned through suffering and leads her readers into a deeper understanding of who God is and why knowing him matters. You won't read this book and then put it on a shelf. You'll keep it handy because you'll refer to its wisdom time and time again.

—GRACE FOX, global worker, international speaker, and author of *Moving from Fear to Freedom: A Woman's Guide to Peace in Every Situation* (gracefox.com)

It seems author Twila Belk has figured out the formula. I can't be courageous until I'm strong. I can't be strong until I'm grateful. And I can't be grateful until I'm still. No wonder she came up with the title *The Power to Be*. This book empowers me to be all those things and more! Twila's trademark style of friend-girl humor and honesty are woven through these scriptural principles and life steps. Her power statements provide intentional affirmations I can take with me the rest of the day, with mind and heart inspired to *be* exactly what God wants.

—KATHY CARLTON WILLIS, author and speaker, God's Grin Gal

Do you struggle with fear, worry, insecurity, or other feelings that hold you back from being who you were created to be? In Twila's relatable and humorous style, she shares from experience and Scripture what it takes to be still, grateful, strong, and courageous. Let her devotions encourage you. Use her practical and powerful tools. And watch what God can do when you turn your attention to him, especially when facing the tough stuff of life.

—GEORGIA SHAFFER, professional certified coach, PA licensed psychologist, author of *A Gift of Mourning Glories: Restoring Your Life after Loss* and *Taking Out Your Emotional Trash*

If you could use a dose of encouragement, strength, faith, and hope, read *The Power to Be* by Twila Belk. This remarkable book offers forty short devotions on choosing to be still, grateful, strong, and courageous. Twila's personal transparency speaks deeply of what she's learned in God's Word about how to apply his truth to the challenges of everyday life. Don't miss this treasure! You'll want to buy several copies to share with friends.

—CAROL KENT, speaker, author of over twenty books, including *He Holds My Hand: Experiencing God's Presence and Protection*, founder of Speak Up for Hope

With wisdom only gained from traveling through many a storm, Twila Belk takes us all on a journey of being. Being still. Being grateful. Being strong. And being courageous. It's a journey like no other, and we're all the better having taken the ride.

—JOANIE AND JENNI BEAVER, co-owners of Positive Note Network (positivenotenetwork.com)

Twila Belk has lived out the truths she writes about in *The Power to Be*. Her trials have taught her how to be still, be grateful, be strong, and be courageous. She is the real deal, and those who read *The Power to Be* will be greatly encouraged to be still, grateful, strong, and courageous as they face their own challenges.

—CAROLE LEWIS, director emeritus
of First Place 4 Health,
author of *Live Life Right Here Right Now*

Once upon a time, a very courageous author decided to write a very powerful book to help readers see the way to be still, grateful, strong, and courageous. In the process, she helped us to recognize God's presence in our lives, develop a thankful heart, and press through our difficulties with the courage of the Lord. Thank you, Twila, for every word!

—LINDA EVANS SHEPHERD, author and speaker,
author of *When You Don't Know What to Pray*,
founder of Right to the Heart Ministries

TWILA BELK

The Power to Be

BE STILL. BE GRATEFUL.
BE STRONG. BE COURAGEOUS.

A 40-DAY DEVOTIONAL

BroadStreet
PUBLISHING

BroadStreet Publishing® Group, LLC
Racine, Wisconsin, USA
BroadStreetPublishing.com

The Power to Be: BE STILL. BE GRATEFUL. BE STRONG. BE COURAGEOUS

Stock or custom editions of BroadStreet Publishing titles may be purchased in bulk for educational, business, ministry, fundraising, or sales promotional use. For information, please email info@broadstreetpublishing.com.

Cover design by Chris Garborg at garborgdesign.com
Typesetting by Katherine Lloyd at theDESKonline.com

Printed in China

18 19 20 21 22 5 4 3 2 1

Now to the King eternal, immortal,
invisible, the only God,
be honor and glory for ever and ever.

Contents

Foreword by Cynthia Ruchti. 1

Introduction 3

PART ONE – *The Power to Be Still*

1 Fix Your Thoughts 7

2 Cease Striving 11

3 Know I AM 14

4 Set Him Always Before You .17

5 Choose to Trust Without Understanding 21

6 Stop Worrying 25

7 Experience God's Embrace. 28

8 Remember God's Track Record. 31

9 Sit in the Quiet with God 35

10 Pray with Thanksgiving 38

PART TWO – *The Power to Be Grateful*

11 Realize the Magnitude of God's Extraordinary Gift 44

12 Appreciate God's Good Gifts 48

13 Acknowledge His Ongoing Benevolence 51

14 Display Gratitude. 55

15 Extend Grace to Others 58

16 Maintain a Grateful Heart 61

17 Gain Perspective 64

18 Engage the WOW Factor 67

19 Pay Attention to the God Stuff. .70
20 Tell Somebody. 74

PART THREE – *The Power to Be Strong*

21 See Yourself as God Sees You 80
22 Reject Negative Messages 84
23 Quit Playing the Comparison Game 88
24 Keep Your Protection in Place. 92
25 Grow Deep Roots. 96
26 Rejoice in Problems and Trials 100
27 Find Joy. 103
28 Wait on the Lord 106
29 Store Up Reserves 109
30 Accept Help and Support from Others 112

PART FOUR – *The Power to Be Courageous*

31 Practice Courage Every Day .118
32 Get Your Eyes off Yourself 121
33 Cling to God's Promises 124
34 Be Mindful of His Presence. .128
35 Consider the Size of Your God. 132
36 Trust and Obey, Then Get out of the Way 136
37 Let God Guide You 140
38 Resolve to Inquire of the Lord 144
39 Execute God's Battle Plan. 147
40 Determine to Trust God Even If. 151

Power Statements 155
About the Author. 161

Foreword

You can tell if a refrigerator or freezer gasket has lost its "oomph" by closing a dollar bill in the door and then attempting to slide the dollar out. If it slips out easily, the gasket isn't holding strongly enough. Time for a replacement. I guess I've owned enough old refrigerators to have picked up that life hack.

Since the moment I first met Twila Belk, I knew that the "gasket" between her and the God she serves is tight. It was easy to love her—easy to consider her an instant sister-friend—because she loves Jesus out loud. It's written all over her face and life. And what a life it's been.

Those who've read her writings know they resonate with unflappable joy wrung out of the sometimes frightening, sometimes devastating, always challenging adventures she has faced and is still facing. She refuses hip-waders, because the burrs that cling to her clothing as she journeys and the mud in life's ditches give her more reason to praise the One who turns burrs into blessings and lovingly washes the mud away with a rough towel tied about his waist, a basin at his side, and our feet in his hands.

Few writers are as skilled as Twila at taking the ordinaries of life and drawing out of them the profound truths that propel us forward on our journey of faith. In *The Power to Be*, she once again invites her readers to step into the pages of Scripture to discover its application for our daily experiences.

Her power statements shift our thinking from "if only" to "I will." Refreshing, uplifting, but compellingly authentic, Twila Belk's *The Power to Be* belongs not only on bookshelves but close to the heart.

Cynthia Ruchti

Speaker and multiple award-winning author of more than twenty books, including *A Fragile Hope* and *As My Parents Age* (cynthiaruchti.com)

Introduction

The power to be. Who doesn't want power? And who doesn't want to be still, grateful, strong, and courageous? Especially with all the challenges we face in life. It *is* possible to have that kind of power, and I hope the book you're holding in your hands (or viewing on a screen) right now will help you discover how.

As I wrote the forty chapters in this devotional, I noticed three recurring messages. The better we are at doing these three things, the more successful we'll be in our pursuit of the power to be: (1) knowing God, (2) trusting God, and (3) keeping our attention on the right things. You'll see how they weave together as you work your way through the book.

In each chapter I've included two features to reinforce the principles and truths I mentioned in the individual readings—a power statement and questions for reflection.

The power statements are positive declarations you can make. Repeat them as often as necessary. The more you say them, the more they'll get into your heart and mind, and the more you'll live them out. Post them in strategic places where they'll remind you that you have the power to be. For your convenience, a compiled list of all forty is included after the last section.

The questions are another tool to enhance the main points of the readings. They're prompters for reflection and writing. You might choose to do something else, such as have a conversation with God. I love to do that, and if that's the direction you take, I know you'll be blessed.

I pray that God will speak to you in specific ways on specific days through this book. My hope is that you will finish with an improved understanding of what a great God we have, and that you will be inspired to know him and trust him more and more each day.

May the Lord bless you and keep you. May the Lord make his face shine on you and be gracious to you. May the Lord turn his face toward you and give you peace. And may he show you that you have the power to be still, grateful, strong, and courageous, if you keep your eyes on him.

Twila Belk

PART ONE

The Power to Be Still

Being still is born out of relationship.
It comes from knowing and trusting I AM.

1

Fix Your Thoughts

And now, dear brothers and sisters, one final thing.
Fix your thoughts on what is true, and honorable, and right,
and pure, and lovely, and admirable. Think about things that are
excellent and worthy of praise. Keep putting into practice all you
learned and received from me—everything you heard from me
and saw me doing. Then the God of peace will be with you.
Philippians 4:8–9 NLT

Be still. That's easier said than done, isn't it? Sometimes I wish I could flip on a little "be still" switch to pacify myself, especially when I have days like today. Right now I'm struggling to gain control of my churning insides.

I'm currently dealing with several major life stressors—undergoing treatment for an aggressive breast cancer, caregiving for my husband who has a rare and progressive muscle disease, carrying a huge burden of financial responsibilities, handling concerns about my youngest son's circumstances, and facing a looming book deadline. Add to that, in the last couple of days, both vehicles stopped working, my faithful recliner broke, and wasps are entering the house through the bathroom vent.

Then this morning, after putting in many hours on a special project for a person I greatly respect, I received a harsh email rather than a thank-you for my hard work. Reading that email, while being physically and mentally exhausted, pushed me into a not-so-good place. I turned into an emotional mess. Although the person apologized a few hours after sending it, my memory naturally wants to replay the narrative again and again, which agitates my spirit more and more.

And here I am with the task of telling people how to be still. Seriously?

I've learned over the years that God likes to give me plenty of opportunities to become well-versed in my topic. And this is one of those times. So after much consideration, I decided I need to change topics. I want to be well-versed in something else! (Perhaps I'll change it to "How to be happy with a million dollars while living in the Caribbean and looking great in a bikini.")

For now, I'm reverting to self-talk mode. "Breathe in. Breathe out. Calm down, Twila. It's time to remind yourself of the sermons you so readily give to others." In other words, I'm giving myself a pep talk to practice what I preach.

And one of the important truths I like to remind people of is this: whatever we focus on becomes magnified.

If I keep my attention on my problems and heartaches (or hurtful words), they become overwhelming to me and tend to control my life. But if I fix my thoughts on God, he becomes magnified in my heart and mind, and I'm reminded of who he is and what he's able to do. My attitude changes, and my unsettled spirit quiets down. It takes resolve, but it's so worthwhile.

Philippians 4:8–9 encourages us to think about whatever is true, noble, right, pure, lovely, admirable, excellent, or praiseworthy. If we put that kind of thinking into practice, peace will be ours.

Lord, when the pressures of life become too much for me, and my circumstances are the foremost thing on my mind, I become stressed and overwhelmed. Would you help me to fix my thoughts on you? I want you to be magnified, not the stuff I'm going through. You are excellent and worthy of praise. You are able to calm my agitated spirit. You are the giver of peace. Thank you for being with me.

POWER STATEMENT

I have the power to be still. Rather than dwelling on my circumstances and letting them overwhelm me, I will fix my thoughts on God.

REFLECTION AND RESPONSE

Isaiah 26:3 says, "You will keep in perfect peace all who trust in you, all whose thoughts are fixed on you!" (NLT). What have your thoughts been fixed on lately? What current issues are keeping you from being still?

2

Cease Striving

"Cease striving and know that I am God; I will be exalted among the nations, I will be exalted in the earth."
Psalm 46:10 NASB

The words in Psalm 46:10 are familiar to many of us: "Be still and know that I am God." The New American Standard version uses the words "cease striving" rather than "be still," which means to let go or relax.

Months ago, on a day when the heaviness of life and responsibilities seemed particularly oppressive to me, I realized I had to let it go—cease striving for control—and relax in God's capable hands. I had a conversation with him that went like this:

"I'm feeling weary of the battle, Lord. Weary of trying to keep my head above water. Weary of trying to hold it all together. I can't do it on my own. I don't know what the answers are, Lord, but I know who the answer is. I must rely on you. You are the one who holds things together.

"Circumstances are beyond my control. I can't control my income. I can't control the bills. I can't control the health issues. I can't control how I feel. I can't control what other people do. I can't control anything. But I *can* choose to trust you, the one who *can* control all things. The one who knows what's going on in my life. The one who cares and loves and knows what's best for me.

"I choose to remember your promises to me. I choose to remember that you are Provider. I choose to remember that you work in creative ways, ways that are beyond my imagination. I choose to remember that you have good plans, plans to prosper me and not harm me. I choose to remember that regardless of the situation, you are big enough to handle it."

That was a freeing experience for me.

Psalm 46:10 in the Amplified version goes like this: "Be still and know (recognize, understand) that I am God." Here's the way I like to translate it. "Get this into your mind and heart: I AM God. I AM I AM. Once you know that—really know, recognize, and understand that—you can rest."

Knowing God and trusting God go hand in hand. If he can speak the world into being; hang the sun, moon, and stars in the sky; calm turbulent seas; bring life through virgin and barren wombs; make the lame walk; give sight to the blind; raise the dead; cause demons to tremble; and rule over all things, he can certainly take care of us, can't he?

Nothing we face is outside the limits of God's control. Let's rest in that truth. And let's repeat it often.

God, when I think about who you are—Creator God and author of life, the God who rules over all things, the God who loves me beyond measure, the God who knows me better than I know myself—I can cease striving and relax in your capable hands. You are aware of what's going on, you understand what I need, and you are fully capable of taking care of me. I release any control I thought I had and put my trust in you.

POWER STATEMENT

Because I know God, I can cease striving for control. I trust him to take care of my needs.

REFLECTION AND RESPONSE

What does Psalm 46:10 mean to you? What do you know about God, and how does knowing that make it possible for you to be still?

3

Know I AM

God said to Moses, "I AM WHO I AM. ...
This is my name forever, the name you shall call me
from generation to generation."
Exodus 3:14–15

When I read the verse "Be still and know that I am God," my mind automatically interprets it this way: "Be still and know I AM."

I AM is a powerful statement. It's also God's name.

In a conversation God had with Moses in Exodus 3:14–15, he told him that his name is I AM WHO I AM. He also pointed out that it was his forever name, and it should be remembered throughout all generations.

Earlier in the same chapter, God made a few noteworthy comments regarding his people in Egypt: (1) "I've seen their misery." (2) "I've heard them crying." (3) "I'm concerned about their suffering." (4) "I've come to rescue them."

Moses and the people of Israel needed a reminder that God hadn't forgotten them and that he was big enough to handle their problems. That reminder is important for us too, because we tend to forget truth when immersed in uncomfortable circumstances.

We live in a different time, but God is the same. He sees our misery. He hears our cries. He's concerned about our suffering. And he will rescue us.

When God calls himself I AM, his message for us is this: "I AM sufficient. I AM able. I AM faithful. I AM trustworthy. I AM the God of details. I AM God of the impossible. I AM always with you. I AM comforter. I AM counselor. I AM healer. I AM sustainer. I AM the one who created you and knows you better than you know yourself. I AM your provider. I AM your strength. I AM your shield. I AM your hiding place. I AM your burden bearer. I AM your source of peace, joy, hope, and rest. I AM your all in all. I AM love. I AM life. Besides that, I AM all-powerful, I AM all-seeing, I AM all-knowing, and I AM accessible. I AM WHO I AM."

I may not retain everything I learned in elementary school, but I do remember that "I AM" is present tense. And knowing that God's name is present tense gives me a sense of peace. When he says I AM, he means that's who he is right now. Today. Time makes no difference in who he was, is, or will be.

As we get to know him through his Word, our personal relationship, our experience, and the testimony of others, we realize that he is and will be all that we need.

He's a God of presence. He's a God of promise.

Know I AM and be still.

I AM WHO I AM, how I love your name, and how grateful I am that you're my God! Your name is filled with promise. Because you are always present, I have no need to worry or fear. You are and will be all I need for each day. You're the same yesterday, today, and forever. And because you never change, I can trust you to be the same big God for me that you were to Moses and the Israelites many years ago. I praise you for being all-seeing and all-knowing, and I thank you that nothing in my life escapes your notice or care.

POWER STATEMENT

I AM WHO I AM is a present-tense God. I have no reason to worry or fear because he is with me right now.

REFLECTION AND RESPONSE

What does God's name, "I AM," mean to you, and how does it apply to your current circumstances?

4

Set Him Always Before You

I have set the LORD continually before me;
Because He is at my right hand, I will not be shaken.
Psalm 16:8 AMP

Do you ever forget anything? I do. Sometimes I'll get on an elevator and wonder why I haven't reached my floor. And then I'll discover it's because I hadn't remembered to push the button. I forget where I've put things. I forget the names of my kids. I forget why I went to the other room. And if I'm not careful, I'll forget meaningful dates or events. If I don't keep a sticky note or some sort of reminder in front of me, I'm in trouble.

Several years ago on an August day, I realized how important those reminders were to me. I went about my business as I normally do, but I had a niggling feeling that I was forgetting something. Halfway through the day, I came across a significant document while sorting a stack of papers on my table. It was the first day of school, and I had forgotten to take my kids! Yikes!

Because I hadn't kept that important information at the top of the pile and smack dab in front of my face, I had to put up with friends and school personnel who laughed at me and questioned my mental stability.

"Out of sight, out of mind" is a clichéd expression, but it's proven to be true in my case.

Unfortunately, that's also often the case with many of us regarding our relationship with God. If we don't keep him at the "top of our pile," we forget that he's with us. We forget that he wants to help us. We forget that he is I AM. And because of our forgetfulness, we're troubled needlessly with a load of care.

David wrote the words in Psalm 16:8 shown above. He knew the key to being still (or unshaken) was to have a constant awareness of the Lord's presence.

Here are some of the ways he kept the Lord continually before him:

- Talked honestly with God and carried on a running conversation with him
- Meditated on God's words
- Journaled his thoughts and prayers to God (see the Psalms)
- Passed down his God stories to the next generation
- Sang praises to God
- Proclaimed God's goodness
- Talked to others about God
- Danced before God
- Opened his eyes and heart to notice God at work
- Immersed himself in the truth of God's Word

As with us, life wasn't always easy for David. He faced storms, dealt with wicked people, confronted giants, had to make difficult decisions, and wrestled with inner turmoil. But because he knew God intimately and kept him at the "top of his pile," David was able to trust him. God proved himself to David again and again and will do the same for us.

I have problems with forgetfulness, Lord, but I don't want that to happen when it comes to you. Help me to learn from David and to keep you continually before me. If I do that, I won't be shaken by the worries and cares and troubles of life. With you at the "top of my pile," I'll remember how big you are, how good you are, and how trustworthy you are. Thank you for being at my right hand.

POWER STATEMENT

I will set the Lord always before me. I am unshakable when he is at my right hand.

REFLECTION AND RESPONSE

What kinds of things shake you? How would setting God always before you help you keep from being shaken? What are methods you could use to help you have a constant awareness of God in your life?

5
Choose to Trust Without Understanding

Trust in the LORD with all your heart,
and lean not on your own understanding; in all your ways
acknowledge Him, and He shall direct your paths.
Proverbs 3:5–6 NKJV

I have what many people call a life verse—a portion of Scripture that's especially meaningful to me—and it pops up often as a reminder of what I need to do. It's Proverbs 3:5–6, as shown above.

In two places the passage uses a tiny three-letter word, and that little word carries a big message. It says I'm supposed to trust God with *all* my heart. I'm supposed to acknowledge him in *all* my ways. (The Amplified version puts it like this: "in all your ways know *and* acknowledge *and* recognize Him.")

All. That's a lot, isn't it?

A few other words hit me in a significant way as I was reading the verses one day: *and lean not on your own understanding.* I had an aha moment when I realized that I'm not going to understand everything. I don't *need* to understand everything. The revelation brought me great freedom because many things that have happened in my life are beyond my mental grasp.

For example: I don't understand why …

- my first baby was a miscarriage;
- I had a complex emergency gallbladder surgery when my daughter was three weeks old, and I couldn't carry her for seven weeks;
- my dad died unexpectedly from a brain aneurysm when he was extremely healthy;
- a drunk driver's vehicle crashed into our van on the way home from a church event;
- my mom died in that accident, and my prognosis wasn't good;
- my youngest son spent ten days in intensive care after he was born;
- my other son's appendix ruptured when he was thirteen, and we almost lost him;
- we've often struggled with financial difficulties;
- my husband has a crippling muscle disease, and he's no longer the strong man I married;
- two of my family members have bipolar disorder;
- I was diagnosed with breast cancer;
- we seem to move from crisis to crisis;
- and I certainly don't understand why I have chin hairs!

But what I do understand is this: God says I should trust him and acknowledge him, and then he gives me a promise. If I do that, he will take care of me. He will direct my paths. I'm not left to flounder on my own. What comfort that brings me!

I've learned that rather than focusing on what I don't know or understand, I should turn my attention to what I do know. I know God. I know he loves me. I know he's never failed me. I know he wants what's best for me.

I choose to trust him and acknowledge him without having to understand everything. Will you?

Lord, so often my life doesn't make sense to me, and I try to figure out why things happen the way they do. Thank you for reminding me that I'm not required to understand everything. As you said in Isaiah 55:8, your thoughts are not the same as my thoughts, and your ways are different than mine. What's most important is that I trust you and acknowledge you. I want to do that, Lord, but it's not always easy. Would you help me? I want you to direct my paths.

POWER STATEMENT

Rather than trying to understand everything, I will trust God with all my heart, and I will acknowledge him in all my ways. When I do that, he will make my paths straight.

REFLECTION AND RESPONSE

What are some of the things in your life that don't make sense to you? Make a list and ask God to help you trust him without the need to understand.

6

Stop Worrying

"Will all your worries add a single moment to your life?"
Matthew 6:27 TLB

I was having a rough morning one April several years ago. Just getting over strep throat, I felt frumpy and looked frumpy, and I had a speaking engagement scheduled for that evening. Although I made an appointment for a haircut, I didn't know how I'd pay for it.

The doorbell alerted me to an unexpected visitor on the front stoop. When I opened the door, I saw my friend Ann holding a casserole dish. She had been praying for me and for the event and wanted to provide dinner for my family. As we chatted, I mentioned that I planned to get my hair done in an hour or two.

"Oh, I forgot something in the car," she said on her way to the kitchen counter. "I'll be right back." When she returned, Ann handed me a twenty-dollar bill. I hadn't told her I lacked the money to pay for my haircut, but God did.

At my appointment, my stylist cut and highlighted my hair. Lisa refused payment and said, "I just want to bless you today and invest in your ministry." Not only did she restore me to my natural beauty, but I also came out of her salon feeling mighty fine.

That day I ended up with supper I didn't have to cook, a new hairdo, twenty extra dollars in my pocket, and confidence to make it through the evening. God knew what I needed and took care of it for me.

God knows exactly what you need too.

When life is unstable or we're concerned about needs, we might have a tendency to worry. Jesus talked about that in Matthew 6:25–34. In verse 25, he said, "So my counsel is: Don't worry about *things*—food, drink, and clothes. For you already have life and a body—and they are far more important than what to eat and wear" (TLB).

He suggested that his audience spend time looking at the birds of the air and the lilies of the field to see how wonderfully God cares for them, and he reminded them how much more valuable they are to God. He asked an important question: "Will all your worries add a single moment to your life?" Good point.

Jesus emphasized that the heavenly Father knows his children's needs. And he finished his lesson saying, "And he will give them to you if you give him first place in your life and live as he wants you to. So don't be anxious about tomorrow. God will take care of your tomorrow too. Live one day at a time" (vv. 33–34).

God has met my needs again and again. I've learned (and continue to learn) that worrying does nothing but disquiet my spirit. Seeking God and trusting him each day is what gives me peace.

Heavenly Father, thank you for the wonderful way you provide for me. You've proven again and again that your care package is complete. You know exactly what I need and when I need it. Thank you for reminding me that worry is unproductive. It doesn't add a single moment to my life, yet it causes me a lot of grief. When I look to you, I have peace and joy in knowing how much you love me. Thank you for being my God today, and thank you for being my God tomorrow. With you, I can live one day at a time.

POWER STATEMENT

I have no worries because my heavenly Father knows my needs.

REFLECTION AND RESPONSE

Do you spend more time worrying or trusting God? Think about how God has cared for you in the past. What will you trust him to care for today? For tomorrow?

1

Experience God's Embrace

Whoever dwells in the shelter of the Most High will rest
in the shadow of the Almighty. I will say of the LORD,
"HE IS MY REFUGE AND MY FORTRESS, my God,
in whom I trust."

Psalm 91:1–2

When my son was a toddler, he sometimes became so troubled that his little body would quiver. He'd sob loudly and shed big tears about the terrible trials in his life. As he reached toward me for comfort, I'd pick him up and hold him tightly. Before long, the third and fourth fingers of his right hand would slide into his mouth and he'd start sucking away. He snuggled into my embrace, keeping his head nestled against my chest, and after a while he was as content as could be.

My precious boy was safe and secure and had no burdens or anxieties when he was in my arms. As far as he was concerned, no one could solve his problems or satisfy his needs quite like his mama.

As God's beloved daughter—an adult child who longs for assurance that everything is going to be okay—I often reach out to him in much the same way.

The words of Psalm 91:1–2 remind me that in his shelter is where I'll find rest. They give me a mental picture of being in my heavenly Father's warm embrace. He's my protector. My hiding place. My sanctuary.

I get a similar vision from Isaiah 41:10, which says: "So do not fear, for I am with you; do not be dismayed, for I am your God. I will strengthen you and help you; I will uphold you with my righteous right hand."

When I change the words around a bit, the meaning deepens for me. "Because I AM is with me, I don't have to fear. Because I AM is my God, I shouldn't be dismayed. Because I AM strengthens me and helps me, I have all I need. Because I AM holds me in his arms, I am at ease."

These verses are beautiful reminders that when the storms of life threaten us, or we face troubles of many kinds, we can reach our arms up to our heavenly Father, the one who calls himself I AM. He pulls us into his warm embrace and lays our head against his breast. With his every heartbeat, our spirit hears, "I love you, I love you, I love you." And we quickly realize that his heart beats for us.

There we dwell, under his shelter, covered by his almighty shadow, where we're out of harm's way. It's a place of solace and relief. We're free from the worries, fears, and disturbances of life.

That's what God wants for us. He longs to hold us close.

When was the last time you reached for his embrace?

Oh God, how I love the warmth and comfort of your embrace. Your arms are strong and calming, and peace resides there. There's no other place I'd rather be. Thank you for answering when I cry out to you. Thank you for being with me in times of trouble. Thank you for your constant readiness to scoop me up and hold me close. I love you, Lord, and I rejoice in the rest that comes from dwelling in you. I don't know what I'd do without your almighty presence in my life. You are my refuge and fortress, my God in whom I trust.

POWER STATEMENT

Almighty God is my refuge and fortress. I can find rest in his warm embrace.

REFLECTION AND RESPONSE

Can you picture yourself in God's embrace? What does that look like to you? What does he say to you and do for you while you're there?

8

Remember God's Track Record

"I will remember the deeds of the LORD; yes, I will remember
your miracles of long ago. I will consider all your works and
meditate on all your mighty deeds. Your ways, God, are holy.
What god is as great as our God? You are the God who
performs miracles; you display your power among the peoples."
Psalm 77:11–14

In the Old Testament, God told the Israelites many times, "Don't forget the things you've experienced. Don't forget what you've seen me do." It's an instruction we need to heed as well.

When we're stuck in the vise grip of life and feeling intense pressure, we have a tendency to forget about anything except our current circumstances. The pain, the fear, the burdens, the weariness, the worry, or whatever, becomes foremost in our minds. Even the Bible greats had problems with this. Take Moses, for example.

Moses knew God intimately and was called God's friend. He had seen God work in one supernatural way after another, miracle after miracle. He experienced God at the burning bush and was there when God opened the Red Sea for the multitude to cross on dry ground. He saw the cloud that led the people by day and the pillar of fire that led them by night.

He met with God on the mountain and received the commandments. He took in God's marvelous provision of manna and so much more.

Then something strange happened. I won't go into all the details, but Numbers 11 tells about how the people got so sick of manna that they grumbled and wailed and complained to Moses. God became exceedingly angry with the Israelites because of their ungrateful behavior.

A troubled Moses—frustrated, exhausted, and weighed down beyond what he could bear—didn't hold anything back as he talked with God about the situation. God promised Moses that he'd send meat. Lots and lots of meat. So much meat that they'd eat and eat and eat until it came out of their nostrils and they'd loathe it.

Now, here's the part that caught me by surprise. Moses doubted God's ability and disputed his promise. He asked, "How is that possible?"

God responded with, "When did I become weak?"

Isn't it amazing God had to ask that question?

Moses' forgetting God's track record seems unbelievable to me. Yet we can be the same way when we're mentally and physically drained, feeling defeated, or in an uncomfortable spot.

The lesson I get out of this is that HOW something is going to happen isn't important, but the WHO we're coming to with our problems is. If we remember who God is and the supernatural power he has, we can bring our impossible-looking circumstances to him without questioning how. Our job is to trust that he is able.

I want to be like the psalmist who said, "I will remember

the deeds of the LORD; yes, I will remember your miracles of long ago." When I remember what God has done for me (or for others) in the past, I can trust him for today and tomorrow. You can too.

Lord, I confess that sometimes when I'm weary, or overly taxed, or in an impossible-looking situation, I forget that you are able. I forget how you've provided and performed in the past. I forget that I can lay out all of my problems before you and leave them in your hands. Would you help me remember to not forget? I want to keep my heart and mind and eyes turned to you, my all-powerful, loving, and trustworthy God.

POWER STATEMENT

I can trust God today and tomorrow because he has shown me his ability in the past.

REFLECTION AND RESPONSE

Reflect on the different impossible-looking circumstances God helped you (or someone else you know) get through in the past. How did he provide? How did he guide? What did he do? How does remembering those things help you to trust him for your current situation? What helps you remember?

9
Sit in the Quiet with God

*"Come with me by yourselves to a quiet place
and get some rest."*

Mark 6:31

In the craziness that is our life—the hurrying, scurrying, busyness, and chaos—we can become so accustomed to the surrounding noise that we feel uncomfortable without it, and we fail to take advantage of time to just sit with nothing distracting us.

Years ago I had a revelation. As I sat in the solitude of my bedroom and gave thought to what I could hear, I realized that even the stillness wasn't so quiet after all. I had become so used to the cacophony that I was able to shut it out.

Right now, while I'm writing this, I'm in a room by myself. I'm ignoring the noises whirling around me because I'm focused on my manuscript and my ears aren't honed in. But when I intentionally stop and listen, I can separate the blended sounds that I've disregarded. I hear a train's rumble in the distance. The tick, tick, ticking of my clock. The wind. Tree limbs whipping. My laptop's fan. The house creaking. A bird's claws scraping against the siding. A truck's engine. A bulldozer shifting metal parts at a nearby house construction. The heater turning on and off.

I'm amazed at everything I can hear when I tune in. And

when I tune in just right, I can even hear the voice of the Lord. Not in an audible way, but in my spirit.

I talk to God a lot throughout the day, but the sweetest times I have are those when I sit in my recliner and it's just me, my laptop, and my heavenly Father in the quiet. The door is closed to remove distractions, and my chair becomes a secret sanctuary. Sometimes, hours can pass as I sit in his presence talking and listening. I use my laptop to journal what I say to him and what I sense he's saying to me.

I share my heart with him. My gratitude, my praise, my troubles, my concerns, my joys, my dreams, my desires, my questions, my daily stuff, and even my silliness. And he responds intimately and tenderly, as any loving father would to his precious child. I like to think of this as spending time on God's lap.

When I reluctantly crawl off of his lap to face whatever is next, I'm fortified. I'm at peace. I have reassurance that I can trust him for everything.

In the Gospels, we see how important times like these were for Jesus. He often slipped away to a special place where he could rest and commune with his Father alone. Early in the mornings. After he got bad news. After pouring himself out in ministry to others. After exhausting himself navigating huge crowds.

That's where he drew his strength. That's where he got centered. That's where he found rest. And that's where we'll find ours. In the quiet with the Father.

Heavenly Father, I love the precious moments I have alone with you. Thank you for welcoming me into your presence. Thank you for the sweet peace and rest that come from spending time there. Thank you for allowing me to share whatever is on my heart, and thank you for the loving ways you respond. Whenever I take time to sit on your lap, I'm fortified and refreshed. You assure me that you're in control. I'm grateful for the privilege of being your child.

POWER STATEMENT

When I sit in the quiet with God, I find rest for my soul.

REFLECTION AND RESPONSE

As you're sitting here, listen to the noises around you. What do you hear? As you tune in, can you hear God's voice? Take this time to journal your thoughts to him and write what you believe he is saying to you.

10
Pray with Thanksgiving

Do not be anxious about anything, but in every situation,
by prayer and petition, with thanksgiving,
present your requests to God. And the peace of God,
which transcends all understanding,
will guard your hearts and your minds in Christ Jesus.
Philippians 4:6–7

The first words in Philippians 4:6 are *don't be anxious about anything*. We might be tempted to read those and say, "What do you mean don't be anxious about anything? Can't you see what's happening in my life right now? Can't you see what's happening in the world? How can I help but be anxious?"

And then as we realize it was the apostle Paul who penned the words—when he was in prison and his life was at stake—we decide that maybe he knows something we don't.

Here's how the New Living Translation puts Philippians 4:6–7: "Don't worry about anything; instead, pray about everything. Tell God what you need, and thank him for all he has done. Then you will experience God's peace, which exceeds anything we can understand. His peace will guard your hearts and minds as you live in Christ Jesus."

Instead of being anxious, we're encouraged to talk to God about everything and to let him know what we need. And while we're doing that, we're supposed to thank him.

Thank him. Really? Again, that can seem like unrealistic advice. As we're praying and presenting our requests before God, we're often doing so out of a defeated mind-set. We might be steeped in pain or feeling weary or discouraged, and we can't help but concentrate on our circumstances. How does the thanksgiving come in?

Oswald Chambers said, "We have to pray with our eyes on God, not on the difficulties." This is what I've learned: Thanksgiving puts the focus on what we have rather than what we lack. On God's character rather than our shortcomings. On God's sufficiency rather than our insufficiencies. On God's ability rather than our impossible-looking situations.

Thanksgiving transfers the heavy load from us to God, our burden bearer. It changes our attitude, gives clarity of mind, and lightens our spirits. It causes us to experience the peace of God, which transcends all understanding.

I like to think of it this way: thanksgiving is the gateway to peace.

When we focus on him and praise him in the midst of whatever we're going through, and when we live in the center of his will, he brings a sense of tranquility to our soul. The turmoil, worries, and what-ifs that would otherwise overwhelm us are stilled.

A picture that comes to my mind is of a mama bird and her babies nestled securely in the cleft of a rocky mountainside, chirping their cheerful melodies as a fierce storm rages around them.

It's not always easy to do, but as I've put praying with thanksgiving into practice, I've experienced how my attention turns away from my anxiety-inducers to God. And before long, I sense his loving arms enveloping me in a warm embrace. It's like a balm to my soul. I'm able to rest in God's nest in the midst of distress with a song of thanksgiving on my heart.

God, I don't like the way my insides churn when the stress of my situation becomes too much for me to handle. Sometimes I feel like having a breakdown and sinking into oblivion. But the reality is that I can't change what's happening, and I can't hide. Rather than letting anxiety torment me, I come to you. Thank you for your care and concern. Thank you for your goodness, faithfulness, and love. Thank you that nothing going on in my life is too big for you to handle or too small for your attention. Thank you for changing my perspective as I focus on you, and thank you for your wonderful gift of peace that exceeds understanding.

POWER STATEMENT

I will thank God in spite of my circumstances because thanksgiving puts my focus on him and leads to peace.

REFLECTION AND RESPONSE

What are some of your anxiety-inducers? Write out your requests to God and let him know your needs. Then spend time expressing your praise and thanksgiving to him. Notice how it makes you feel.

PART TWO

The Power to Be Grateful

Gratitude is an offering precious
in the sight of God, and it is one that the poorest
of us can make and be not poorer but richer
for having made it. (A. W. Tozer)

11

Realize the Magnitude of God's Extraordinary Gift

*"For God so [greatly] loved and dearly prized the world,
that He [even] gave His [One and] only begotten Son,
so that whoever believes and trusts in Him [as Savior]
shall not perish, but have eternal life."*
John 3:16 AMP

Years ago, my mom and I had the privilege of meeting a man named Lawrence at the University of Iowa Hospital. He was there for surgical follow-up. His wife sat in a chair next to his bed, and Mom and I sat on the opposite side, as he told us his fascinating story.

He said that at the age of fifty-eight, he had the heart of a ninety-year-old man. He tried medications, a better diet, exercises, different sleep routines—anything he could to get better on his own—but doctors said his only possibility for recovery was a heart transplant.

Late one March night, he received a life-changing phone call. "Good news, Lawrence," the voice on the other end of the line said, "we finally have the perfect match for you! Pack your bags and get ready to go. An airlift is on the way, and you'll have another heart within a few hours."

He was so excited he could have flown on his own power.

The surgery transformed him. Realizing he had received an extraordinary gift that came at an exorbitant price, his every heartbeat led to an awareness of things previously taken for granted. He had hope for the future, great joy, and a fresh outlook on life.

As Lawrence gave us the details, his emotions came to the surface and he wept uncontrollably. The gratitude he had overwhelmed him. We couldn't help but get teary-eyed too. We understood because this man's body held my dad's heart. Knowing that my dad's death made Lawrence's life possible brought purpose to our pain, and Mom and I were able to rejoice with him and his wife.

As I reflect on this many years later, I can't help but think about what God, the Giver, has done for us through his Son, Jesus Christ. John 3:16 tells us how God loved us and prized us so much that he allowed his only Son to die so we could live. And Jesus said in John 10:10, "I came that they may have *and* enjoy life, and have it in abundance [to the full, till it overflows]" (AMP).

Because Jesus died, we have the promise of eternal life *and* life to the full right now, if we believe in and trust in him. He gave us an incomparable gift that comes with amazing benefits. That should cause us to be continuously grateful.

Here are a few ways we can live out our gratitude:

- Love him with all our heart, soul, mind, and strength, and love our neighbor as we love ourselves (see Mark 12:30–31).
- Get to know what would bring him pleasure and do it. (Through communication with him and reading his Word, we'll discover what that is.)

- Put him in the proper place in our lives.
- Give him praise and brag on him to others.
- Trust him in every situation.
- And celebrate his wonderful gifts.

Imagine the delight we'd bring him.

God, as I think about the cost of your extraordinary gift, I'm humbled. That you would allow your Son to die so I could live in a forever relationship with you is hard for me to grasp. Thank you for your amazing love. Thank you for your forgiveness. Thank you that Jesus' death opened the doors of communication with you. Thank you for the promise of eternal life. Thank you that your gift means I can have abundant life right now. God, I have so much to be thankful for. May my gratitude show in the way I love you, live for you, and trust you. And may I bring you delight.

POWER STATEMENT

God has given me an extraordinary gift that came at an exorbitant price. How can I not be grateful?

REFLECTION AND RESPONSE

What does John 3:16 mean to you? Can God tell you're grateful for what he's done? What does a life lived in gratitude for God's extraordinary gift look like to you?

12

Appreciate God's Good Gifts

Every good and perfect gift is from above,
coming down from the Father of the heavenly lights,
who does not change like shifting shadows.

James 1:17

A big present sat under the tree for me one Christmas many years ago, and I knew exactly what it was. The gift I had requested. The gift for which I had spelled out specific details. Color. Price. Where to purchase it. I had even circled a picture of the item in the store catalog.

When the time came to open the package, I tore into the wrapping paper like a wild woman, popped open the top of the box, and gleefully reached inside to pull out my new—

Wait a minute. That's not what I wanted!

My hands held the most horrendous lamp I had ever seen—dark brown with white, frosting-like globs decorating it—nothing at all like the classy, neutral-colored lamp from JC Penney that would look great with my new blue carpet and curtains.

"Honey, you shouldn't have gone to so much trouble," I said to my husband with all sincerity.

"I got a really good deal on it. It cost me only five bucks."

To his credit, Steve was raised to be thrifty; good deals make him happy. But I wasn't happy that he chose to be thrifty with my Christmas gift that year. Honestly, in that moment I didn't feel especially valued. I wondered why I was worth only five bucks and not something that cost full price.

I've never wondered that about God's gifts.

The gifts this world gives are imperfect. They disappoint. They don't last. They break. They deteriorate. They lose their usefulness. They depreciate.

On the other hand, God's gifts are good and perfect. They can't be duplicated. They're exactly what we need. And they're more precious than anything money can buy. They demonstrate his extravagant love for us.

If we open our eyes and pay attention, we'll notice that we're immersed in God's countless physical gifts. They're everywhere, and they're ours to enjoy. He also bestows on us innumerable spiritual blessings.

Ephesians 1:3 says, "All praise to God, the Father of our Lord Jesus Christ, who has blessed us with every spiritual blessing in the heavenly realms because we are united with Christ" (NLT). Did you notice the word *every*?

God's wonderful gifts aren't contingent on anything we've done. They're available to us because of Jesus. And the best part of all is that he "does not change like shifting shadows," as James 1:17 says. He's consistent in his giving.

Consider God's physical gifts. Ponder his spiritual blessings. How is it possible that he values us so much? How is it possible that he's so generous with us? How is it possible that we fail to appreciate all he offers?

When was the last time you thanked him?

All praise goes to you, my lavish, giving God, who bestows every good and perfect gift and who has given me every spiritual blessing in the heavenly realms. Your gifts are nothing less than the best, and they show how much you cherish me. Thank you for the gift of your presence, your provision, your love, your promises, your purposes and plans, life and light, wisdom, your Holy Spirit, grace, mercy, compassion, forgiveness. Thank you for peace, joy, and hope. Oh God, I could go on and on, and my list would never end because you are a consistent, generous giver. May I never stop counting my many blessings and offering praise to you.

POWER STATEMENT

I will consistently thank God because God consistently gives. Daily I will count and appreciate his many blessings.

REFLECTION AND RESPONSE

Start making a running list of God's good gifts and spiritual blessings, and thank him for how they've impacted your life. Add to your list as things come to mind.

13

Acknowledge His Ongoing Benevolence

*But He has said to me, "My grace is sufficient for you
[My lovingkindness and My mercy are more than enough—
always available—regardless of the situation]; for [My] power
is being perfected [and is completed and shows itself most
effectively] in [your] weakness." Therefore, I will all the more
gladly boast in my weaknesses, so that the power of Christ
[may completely enfold me and] may dwell in me.*

2 Corinthians 12:9 AMP

My friends and I had just finished eating at the mall's food court and got up to go. Each of us cleared our areas and disposed of our plates and wrappers—except for one. He walked away, his trash and tray still on the table.

"Aren't you going to deal with your garbage?" I asked.

"Hey, I paid such an exorbitant price, I don't need to do anything else," he said.

His response didn't set well with me, and I shot back with, "I'm sure glad God doesn't feel that way."

With my friend's comment, I had an instant reminder of what the apostle Paul said in Romans 8:32: "He who did not spare his own Son, but gave him up for us all—how will he not also, along with him, graciously give us all things?"

After paying an unimaginable price on our behalf, God

didn't say, "I'm done now. I don't have to do anything more." Instead, he continues to give. He continues to love. He continues to pour into our lives. His gifts are always available.

Hymn-writer Annie Johnson Flint, inspired by Paul's words in 2 Corinthians 12:9 above, penned a beautiful reminder that God "giveth and giveth and giveth again" in her heartfelt and timeless song *He Giveth More Grace* (now in the public domain). She was intimately familiar with heartache, trials, and tribulations, but she was also intimately familiar with the never-ending goodness of her God. She experienced and acknowledged God's benevolence in her life through her suffering. Here's how she expressed it:

He giveth more grace when the burdens grow greater,
He sendeth more strength when the labors increase;
To added afflictions He addeth His mercy,
To multiplied trials, His multiplied peace.

When we have exhausted our store of endurance,
When our strength has failed ere the day is half done,
When we reach the end of our hoarded resources
Our Father's full giving is only begun.

Fear not that thy need shall exceed His provision,
Our God ever yearns His resources to share;
Lean hard on the arm everlasting, availing;
The Father both thee and thy load will upbear.

His love has no limits, His grace has no measure,
His power no boundary known unto men;
For out of His infinite riches in Jesus
He giveth, and giveth, and giveth again.

I too am a recipient of God's always available grace, his limitless love, and his abundant strength, mercy, and peace. I don't know where I'd be without it. I've learned that it's possible to be grateful and to boast in my weaknesses because the weaknesses are what's showcased God's giving nature.

As the song says, "When we reach the end of our hoarded resources, our Father's full giving is only begun." It doesn't matter to him that he's already paid an exorbitant price.

God, how can I not be grateful for the many ways you've poured out your love on me? You know just what I need and when I need it. Thank you for your marvelous gift of grace and strength. Thank you for mercy and peace. Thank you for giving me endurance. Thank you for your provision. Thank you that your everlasting arms never tire of holding me up. And thank you for giving, and giving, and giving again. I'm blessed beyond measure.

POWER STATEMENT

I will gratefully acknowledge God's goodness in my life, even in the midst of trials and afflictions. My needs will never exceed his provision.

REFLECTION AND RESPONSE

Reread the words to the song above, and think about the times you've experienced God's grace or strength or mercy or peace. Have you acknowledged these as God's gifts in your life? What are some of the things God's given to you again and again and again?

14

Display Gratitude

*Each of you should use whatever gift you
have received to serve others, as faithful stewards
of God's grace in its various forms.*

1 Peter 4:10

When our daughter was a freshman in high school, my husband and I had the perfect Christmas present in mind for her—a new flute. Laney was an exceptional musician but still using her beginner instrument, and it was time for us to invest in her giftedness. We did our research, visited several music stores, asked questions, and finally settled on a Pearl open-holed flute with a silver head. She'd be able to use it for the rest of her life.

Yes, it was pricey and took a while to pay for it, but it was worth every penny. Why? Because after she received it, she cried, screamed, jumped up and down, and reacted in lots of other Laneyfied ways that showcased her middle name of Joy. Because she practiced for hours on end. Because she played it just for fun. Because the song in her heart came out through her flute and up to heaven in a beautiful melody that made God and her parents smile.

Laney displayed her gratitude every time she performed, and she allowed the gift to go on by blessing and inspiring countless others through her concerts and music ministry at church.

Likewise, I have someone who's invested in me. I first met

Cec Murphey—a veteran author, highly respected in the publishing industry—at the Write to Publish Conference in 1998. I'd never been to a writers conference before, didn't know much about the publishing process, and felt clueless about many things. During an after-hours critique group session, we connected over a story I wrote called "Toenail Love." It was a divine appointment.

Cec saw something special in me and suggested we stay in touch after the conference. I complied—for a while. A few years later, I met him again. "Why did you stop emailing me?" he asked.

"You have thousands of people who want your attention. Why would you want me to bother you?"

He looked straight into my eyes, bobbed his index finger at me, and said, "Because I see you as one of God's champions. I sponsor champions."

Over the years since then, he's mentored me, employed me, opened new doors for me, provided opportunities for me, introduced me to key people, and allowed me to learn the publishing industry from the inside out. I'm honored to be a beneficiary of his favor.

To show my gratitude for his kindness and goodness, I brag on him whenever I can, I serve him faithfully and with excellence, I share the gifts I've developed with others, and I pour into others the way he's poured into me. I don't do it because it's expected, but because it brings me—and the one who's invested in me—joy.

Wouldn't our generous God, who has invested so much in us, be delighted if we responded to his abundant blessings in the same four ways? Being grateful involves more than a simple thank-you. It should be on display.

Lord, I praise you for your goodness and kindness. I praise you for your generous nature. I praise you for the countless ways you've shown me that you believe in me. Thank you for being my champion and investor. Thank you for valuing and gifting me. I'm amazed and humbled to be a beneficiary of your favor. It's my honor to serve you, to share the gifts you've given me with others, and to love as you've loved me. I do it with joy. May the song in my heart and my offerings of gratitude bring you pleasure.

POWER STATEMENT

To show my gratitude for God's kindness and goodness, I will brag on him whenever I can, serve him faithfully and with excellence, share the gifts he's given me with others, and love others as he's loved me.

REFLECTION AND RESPONSE

How has God invested in you? What gifts has he given you? In what specific ways can you display your gratitude for all he's done?

15

Extend Grace to Others

Bearing graciously with one another, and willingly forgiving
each other if one has a cause for complaint against another;
just as the Lord has forgiven you, so should you forgive.
Colossians 3:13 AMP

I saw a meme on Facebook that said, "Gratitude is our ability to see the grace of God, morning by morning, no matter what else greets us in the course of the day." One October many years ago, the grace and gratitude connection became very real to me.

The crisp fall evening was perfect for a square dance in the country—starry sky, lively music, hay bales, yummy food, sweet fellowship. A night to remember in so many ways. My husband, our six-year-old daughter, my mom, and I had a delightful time with church members and friends. Shortly before the party ended, we said our goodbyes so we could get Mom home.

A few minutes later, our full-size conversion van lay upside down in a ditch from the impact of a speeding car. A drunk driver. We had planned to deliver Mom to her Pleasant Valley address. Instead, God welcomed her in heaven, and doctors didn't expect me to live.

In an instant, our lives changed dramatically. I lost my best friend, our kids no longer had their grandma, we had to rely on others' help at home and with our businesses, and I entered into a several-month period of recovery. Yet in the midst of the shock, healing, and grieving, my husband and I were able to forgive the man whose choices caused this unnecessary tragedy.

As you may know, the ability to forgive doesn't come naturally. When someone has wronged us, we want to retaliate, or hate the person forever. Many times I've thought about how we were able to release those feelings, especially after having to endure the man's false accusations and a horrible court trial experience. I can honestly say it was only because of God's grace. During all this, God gave me a glimpse of how much he had forgiven me. To not offer the same gift to another would be like saying I was better than God.

It may seem strange, but extending grace to those who've wronged us is an act of gratitude for the grace we've received from God. We are, in a way, saying, "Thank you, God, for your kindness and mercy. Thank you for your unmerited favor. Thank you for your unconditional love."

And whether the person acknowledges our gift—or even has awareness of it—we do it more for ourselves. It's a gesture that brings freedom. By letting go and pardoning others' actions, we're able to move forward with our lives. We're not stuck in the rut of bitterness, resentment, anger, and all those negative feelings that imprison us.

Over the years I've learned that grace can't be explained; it can only be experienced. And when we realize the amazing gift we've received, we can't help but be grateful. God sees our hearts and smiles when we're able to extend the same grace to others.

No, it doesn't make sense, but it feels so good. And that makes me grateful all the more.

God, your grace is amazing. I don't deserve it, yet you so readily pour it out on me. Thank you for your gift of forgiveness, and thank you for making it possible for me to extend forgiveness to others. It's not always easy to do, Lord, but it brings such a feeling of relief and reminds me of the mercy and grace I've received from you. Regardless of what happens during my days, would you help me to always see your grace? I may not be able to explain what it is, but I sure know it when I experience it. And I'm eternally grateful.

POWER STATEMENT

Because God has extended his grace to me, I will gratefully extend grace to others.

REFLECTION AND RESPONSE

Have you ever thought about the grace and gratitude connection? How does receiving grace make you grateful? Is there anyone you need to forgive right now? Ask God for the grace to make that possible.

16
Maintain a Grateful Heart

Always be joyful. Never stop praying.
Be thankful in all circumstances, for this is God's
will for you who belong to Christ Jesus.
1 Thessalonians 5:16–18 NLT

I have a wall-hanging in my living room with these words on it: "Happy moments praise God. Difficult moments seek God. Quiet moments worship God. Painful moments trust God. Every moment thank God." It serves as a good reminder of the apostle Paul's words above.

In his letter to the Thessalonians, Paul exhorted them to maintain a grateful heart. As we learn from Acts chapter 16, they're words Paul applied to his own life. (Notice he didn't say to be thankful *for* all circumstances but to be thankful *in* all circumstances.)

Paul and Silas had caused an uproar in Philippi by casting out a spirit in a slave girl. The girl's owners, angry about what they had done, dragged them into the marketplace to face the authorities. The crowd joined in attacking them. After Paul and Silas were stripped and severely flogged, per the magistrate's orders, they were thrown in prison where their feet were fastened in stocks. A jailer guarded them constantly.

Imagine being in their sandals. How would you feel? What would you be thinking about?

Instead of being absorbed in their pain and concentrating

on the unjustness of their punishment, as we might be tempted to do, Paul and Silas lifted their hearts in prayer and praise to God. They sang hymns and expressed thankfulness in an excruciating situation, and the other prisoners listened.

What happened next is amazing. A massive earthquake shook the prison to its foundations. All the doors immediately flew open, and every prisoner's chains fell off. The terrified jailer prepared to kill himself because he couldn't face the shame of having prisoners escape. But Paul shouted to him, "Stop! Don't do it. We're all still here."

Due to Paul and Silas's demonstration of God's grace, the jailer and all who lived in his household came to know the Lord in a personal way. The jailer was so moved and so grateful that he cared for them and washed their wounds, even though it was in the wee hours of the morning.

This story shows that gratitude is a change agent. Not only does it open prison doors, release shackles, and impact relationships, but it has many other benefits as well. Gratitude—redirects our focus to God, reminds us of God's goodness and faithfulness, gives us a new perspective, opens our eyes to things we've taken for granted, increases our awareness, puts a song in our hearts, changes the atmosphere around us, flips negativity into positivity, silences the enemy, diminishes fear, lightens our load, helps our face look better, makes us happier, improves our health, causes people to want to hang out with us, inspires others, and—best of all—it makes God smile.

Are you enjoying the benefits of a grateful heart?

Lord, I'll admit that being thankful in all circumstances seems impossible at times. It's easier to just wallow in my pain or dwell on the unfairness of life. But that's such a slippery slope, Lord! If I allow myself to do that, I'll slide deeper and deeper into the pit of despair. Even though I struggle to turn my thoughts to you, I've learned that the effort is definitely worth it. When I think about your goodness and faithfulness, your power, the gift of your presence, your grace, and so many other things, I can't help but be grateful. Help me to keep my focus on you.

POWER STATEMENT

When I'm thankful in all circumstances, my life changes for the better.

REFLECTION AND RESPONSE

Have you ever struggled with Paul's exhortation to be thankful in all circumstances? What was going on at the time? How would being thankful in the midst of your current situation change your life for the better? What can you thank God for right now?

17

Gain Perspective

What will I give to the LORD [in return] for all His benefits toward me? [How can I repay Him for His precious blessings?]
Psalm 116:12 AMP

A dump isn't a normal place to visit in a foreign country, but when you're involved in a mission trip to Ecuador with the theme of "Never the Same," it's the type of thing you do. I was a chaperone for a team of teenagers, and our ministry one day was to the adults and children who made the heaps of rotting rubbish and discarded trash their home.

As our bus entered the site, the stench overpowered us. We could barely breathe, yet eighty-five families lived there. How is that possible? Our observations messed with our minds. Small cardboard shelters jutted from the mountain range of spoiled food products that were intermingled with soiled diapers, shards of glass, and the broken pieces of people's lives. Garbage trucks arrived with regularity, and as they unloaded their contents, flocks of eager dump dwellers rummaged through the "fresh" goods.

On our way to the location, we had stopped at a market to purchase boxes of basic food staples to take with us. Many of us brought small toiletry items we had collected at home—soap, shampoo, lotions—the type of things hotels provide. While a group of teens and chaperones distributed supplies, others engaged the kids with activities.

We had barely stepped off the bus when a long line formed. Before us stood the most beautiful, filthy, sun-baked people with scraggly hair I had ever seen. Tattered, mismatched clothes hung on their bodies, and a few had feet covered with pitiable shoes they had found among the refuse. The rest were barefoot.

As soon as I opened my bag of toiletry items, hands reached out on all sides of me. A woman with deep creases in her face and dark, longing eyes looked up at me and begged, "*Champú, champú.*" When I gave her a tiny bottle of shampoo, her face beamed as if I had given her the key to Fort Knox.

The whole experience tugged at my heart. I cried out to God, "Oh Lord, please help me to never, ever forget that picture. You've given me so much. I have super-sized bottles of shampoo that I don't even think about. This woman's world became a better place with just an ounce. I have a bed. I have a roof over my head. I have clothes. I have soap and water. I have food—food that goes to waste. Everything these people have comes from a garbage truck." I ended my plea to God with, "May I always maintain a grateful heart."

The rest of the team had a similar revelation. Once back on the bus, many of them removed their shoes and articles of clothing, and they zealously dug through backpacks to find other items they could leave behind as gifts.

We all gained a new perspective that day. Rather than being discontent with what we didn't have, we realized what we did have, and left the dump forever changed.

Oh God, thank you for the gift of perspective! I don't realize how much I have until I see others who have so little. How is it possible that they can display such gratitude for their meager possessions and I act as if I am in need? Forgive me for not acknowledging the abundance of blessings I enjoy every day. Would you give me an awareness of things I tend to take for granted? Would you nudge me to share what I have with others? Would you help me to live in the reality of how blessed I am? I want to have a contented and grateful heart.

POWER STATEMENT

I realize how blessed I am when I open my eyes to all I have.

REFLECTION AND RESPONSE

Take a few minutes to reflect on how much you have, and thank God for the things you normally take for granted. Start an ABC gratitude list, writing down whatever you can think of for each letter of the alphabet. Keep your list going and add to it as you can.

18

Engage the WOW Factor

You thrill me, LORD, with all you have done for me!
I sing for joy because of what you have done.
O LORD, what great works you do!
Psalm 92:4–5 NLT

A few years ago, my husband became a collector, and his hobby brought him almost as much joy and excitement as his three favorite things in life—Whitey's ice cream, Colorado, and the occasional Chicago Cubs win. He would search through newspapers and mailings with Sherlock Holmes' intensity, and when he found what he was looking for, he was giddy. He quickly cut out his prize find and carefully placed it in his wallet to carry with him wherever he'd go, right there with the pictures of his precious children and lovely wife.

It's hard to believe that an oil-change coupon could bring such jubilation to a man's life. But for him, it did. Especially when it meant an oil change for less than ten dollars. He's moved on to other activities now, but remembering his old habit (and some of my own) caused me to do a bit of deep thinking.

Why is it that simple, and even silly, things can lead to delight, yet so often we overlook the special and spectacular that God gives us? Wouldn't God be blessed if we responded to his largess in the same way?

I thought about the times my then-young son Jesse and I played our who-can-find-the-prettiest-tree game. One day, while in the car, we passed an exceptionally beautiful maple that was exploding with vibrant fall colors. Jesse could hardly contain his excitement when he saw it. "WOW, Mom! Look at that tree! It's just like fireworks, but it doesn't have the boom."

That was definitely a WOW moment, one that led to praising God. I pictured God smiling with pleasure as his children marveled at what he had provided for them to enjoy.

Sadly, many of us have forgotten how to engage the WOW factor. We mechanically go about our day-to-day business—or we dawdle in our doldrums—and in the process we become dulled to the amazing handiwork of our creative God. We lose our sense of awe, wonderment, and elation of the things that point us to him.

What would happen if we slowed down and actually became aware of all that surrounds us? Triumphant spring tulips, bursting with life. Birds cheerfully chirping their alleluias. Bushy-tailed squirrels scurrying up trees. A baby's broad, toothless grin. Would we be more apt to acknowledge and appreciate God's involvement in our lives? Would we be more mindful of his love and faithfulness? Would we be more likely to thank him and praise him for who he is and for all he's done?

Rather than taking his gifts for granted, I want to engage the WOW factor. How about you?

Magnificent Creator God, I'm in awe of you. All you've created showcases how powerful and masterful you are. The heavens declare your glory. The earth testifies to your breathtaking artistry. The colors and intricate details of your designs point to an extraordinary God—the God who wants to be intimately involved in my life. When I think of that, I can't help but say "WOW!" May I never become dulled to the beauty of your handiwork, Lord, and may I never lose my sense of wonderment and excitement over the things you made for me to enjoy. I praise you for being an amazing God.

POWER STATEMENT

I will engage the WOW factor and enjoy God's artistry. I will acknowledge God's power and give him praise.

REFLECTION AND RESPONSE

What's your response to a WOW God?

19

Pay Attention to the God Stuff

Though the fig tree does not bud and there are no grapes on the vines, though the olive crop fails and the fields produce no food, though there are no sheep in the pen and no cattle in the stalls, yet I will rejoice in the LORD, I will be joyful in God my Savior.

Habakkuk 3:17–18

While in the midst of bleak circumstances years ago, I stared out the window and noticed the parched landscape due to a long-lasting drought. *That's just the way our life is right now. Everything's dried up.*

I thought about my husband's fall from a ladder at work, leaving his arm seriously damaged and him without income. I thought about the loss of my medical transcription job because the neurosurgeons' personnel started doing it in-house. I thought of the piles of bills and threat of foreclosure on our house. So many trials happening at once.

The picture in the physical realm represented lack, yet in the spiritual realm, God kept reminding me of his abundance. He promised again and again that "the rain is coming," and he continually assured me of his presence, purposes, and plans. In one of my conversations with God, he strongly impressed upon my heart to "keep a tab on the God stuff" I experience, so I started to intentionally document anything out of the ordinary that came to us. Here are just a few of the too-nu-merous-to-mention blessings God provided in less than two months' time.

Monetary gifts: Multiple cash gifts in various amounts received at church. $60 in the mail from an anonymous per-son who loves seeing Jesus in me. $200 in the mail with a note, "The Lord told me to send this to you." An envelope taped to the van with $100 inside and this message, "To: Twila, From: The prompting of the Holy Spirit." A visitor who left $200 and said, "I just wanted you to know I've been praying for you." $60 stuck in my purse by an out-of-town guest. $30 found inside laptop computer. A $4 rebate check. Two $500 checks. Two unexpected worker's comp checks. More than $1,000 earned from garage sale. And many other monetary gifts.

Practical gifts: Brakes on the van repaired for one-fourth the normal cost. Gift cards for gas. Free haircuts. Backpack filled with office supplies for college-bound daughter. Presence of church friends during husband's surgery. Help with our young son's needs.

Food gifts: $50 grocery store gift card "from Jesus." A box filled with meat from the butcher. Meals brought to the house. Restaurant gift cards. Homegrown corn and tomatoes (my favorite). Ice cream (my husband's favorite). Three big pack-ages of Oscar Mayer deli meat. Other random food items.

Fun gifts: Several requests for me to speak. A miracle trip to Colorado (my husband's favorite place in the world) with perfect timing for his fiftieth birthday. An opportunity for our daughter to go on a mission trip to Peru.

This list is only a partial picture of the special kindnesses

God poured out on us during the time I "kept a tab on the God stuff." He proved once again how lavish he is and that his care package is complete.

I learned to be more intentionally aware of his gifts and sweet surprises. And because my eyes have been opened to his ongoing goodness, I'm a more grateful person. (And I just gotta tell somebody!)

I rejoice in you, Lord, for you are an amazing God. You thrill me with all you have done! Thank you for the creative ways you provide. Thank you for the people you use to help deliver your gifts. Thank you for reminding me that you are an abundant God, and that even when circumstances look bleak, there's always hope through you. When my eyes are on you, I never have lack. Lord, help me to stay intentionally aware of your gifts and sweet surprises. You've shown me that the more aware I am, the more bounteous the blessings become. I delight in your thoughtful goodness, Lord, and I delight in you.

POWER STATEMENT

With God there is never lack. The more intentionally aware I am, the more bounteous his blessings become.

REFLECTION AND RESPONSE

Ask God to help you be intentionally aware of his gifts and sweet surprises. Start keeping a tab on the "God stuff" and thank him for the way he smiles on you.

20

Tell Somebody

*I will praise the Lord at all times. I will constantly speak
his praises. I will boast only in the Lord; let all who are helpless
take heart. Come, let us tell of the Lord's greatness;
let us exalt his name together.*

Psalm 34:1–3 NLT

Many people know me as the Gotta Tell Somebody Gal. I'm
a writer and speaker who loves braggin' on God. My heart
gets so full of gratitude from what I've seen and heard and
experienced God do in my life that I can't hold it in. It spills
out my mouth.

I have proof of who God is and how big God is. I have
proof of his love and faithfulness. I have proof that he can be
trusted. And I just gotta tell somebody! What makes it so fun
is that the more I brag on God, the more he gives me to brag
about.

The Psalms are full of accounts where the writers had to
"get it out." I can picture David sitting on a hillside or in whatever situation he was in at the time, when all of a sudden the
WOW factor kicks in.

"WOW! God does answer prayer! God does provide!"

"WOW! Isn't that mountain fabulous? Look at those stars!
What amazing handiwork!"

"WOW! God protected me from those big, ugly guys!"

"WOW! God is faithful! He really is here and shows that he cares! He does love me!"

And then I can imagine him saying, "I just gotta tell somebody! I better write this down." I'm convinced that's why we have many of the psalms we do today.

Here are a few of David's and the other psalmists' gotta-tell-somebody moments:

- I will give thanks to you, Lord, with all my heart; I will tell of all your wonderful deeds. (Psalm 9:1)
- I will not die but live, and will proclaim what the Lord has done. (Psalm 118:17)
- But as for me, how good it is to be near God! I have made the Sovereign Lord my shelter, and I will tell everyone about the wonderful things you do. (Psalm 73:28 NLT)
- I will sing of the Lord's great love forever; with my mouth I will make your faithfulness known through all generations. I will declare that your love stands firm forever, that you have established your faithfulness in heaven itself. (Psalm 89:1–2)
- Your awe-inspiring deeds will be on every tongue; I will proclaim your greatness. (Psalm 145:6 NLT)
- My mouth will speak in praise of the Lord. Let every creature praise his holy name for ever and ever. (Psalm 145:21)
- Sing a new song to the Lord! Let the whole earth sing to the Lord! Sing to the Lord; praise his name. Each day proclaim the good news that he saves.

Publish his glorious deeds among the nations. Tell everyone about the amazing things he does. (Psalm 96:1–3 NLT)

Not only do the psalmists tell, proclaim, declare, praise, speak, and sing of their God experiences, but they also encourage us to do the same.

A grateful heart should be heard. Can people hear yours?

God, you are so good and amazing and wonderful that I can't hold it in. I gotta tell somebody! I join David in saying I will praise you at all times. I will constantly speak your praises. I will boast only in you. I will tell of your greatness. I will exalt your name. And I will invite everyone I know to do the same. Lord, you have no equal. You are above and beyond. You are creator, provider, sustainer, equipper, and ruler over all things. You are all-powerful, all-knowing, and all-seeing. You are with me, you carry me, you love me, you welcome me, and you smile upon me. You are compassionate, generous, gracious, merciful, faithful, trustworthy, and strong. I love you, I delight in you, and I rejoice in you. Thank you for putting a song in my heart.

POWER STATEMENT

I will praise the Lord at all times. I will constantly speak his praises. I will tell of the Lord's greatness, and I will encourage others to do the same.

REFLECTION AND RESPONSE

If you were to write a psalm of praise to the Lord, what would it say? What are some of the things you want others to know about God?

PART THREE

The Power to Be Strong

Seek the LORD and his strength;
seek his presence continually!
—1 Chronicles 16:11 ESV

21

See Yourself as God Sees You

I praise you because I am fearfully and wonderfully made;
your works are wonderful, I know that full well.

Psalm 139:14

You are one of God's works, and God's works are wonderful. Do you know that full well?

That's where being strong begins. We can't be strong when our concept of who we are is weak.

So often we allow outside influences, circumstances, past experiences, the things people say, hormones, or even how much sleep we've had to determine how we see ourselves. And that can lead to distorted thinking. It's essential that we know truth and walk in truth. Who we are, our value, and our status are established by God, not by us or anyone else.

Here's a good dose of truth to absorb:

We are fearfully and wonderfully made, unique, created with a divine purpose, cherished, chosen, accepted, called, and constantly thought about *by the God who* oversaw every part of our being, has ordained our days, is familiar with all our ways, knows us by name, perceives our thoughts, has his hand of blessing upon us, numbers the hairs on our head, is mindful of us, cares for us, forgives completely, loves unconditionally, is *for* us rather than against us, welcomes us into his embrace, carries us close to his heart, can be trusted, is always present, wants to use us in big ways, and desires our fellowship.

Regarding our value to God:

Not only are we his handiwork (and he doesn't make junk), but he also showed our true worth when he paid the highest price—the death of his Son—to open the channels of relationship with him. Romans 5:8 says, "But God demonstrates his own love for us in this: While we were still sinners, Christ died for us."

We're so valuable that he knows exactly how many hairs we have, yet the number of his thoughts about us can't be counted. Matthew 10:29–31 tells us this: "Not one sparrow (What do they cost? Two for a penny?) can fall to the ground without your Father knowing it. And the very hairs of your head are all numbered. So don't worry! You are more valuable to him than many sparrows" (TLB). And Psalm 139:17–18 says, "How precious are your thoughts about me, O God. They cannot be numbered! I can't even count them; they outnumber the grains of sand!" (NLT).

Regarding our status with God versus the world's values:

- The world values the outward appearance. God looks at our hearts.
- The world values position. God says we're royalty.
- The world values riches. God made us joint-heirs with Jesus.
- The world values careers. God made us his ambassadors.

- The world values education. God gives us wisdom, knowledge, and understanding.
- The world values social standing. God offers us a relationship with the King of Kings and Lord of Lords.
- The world values success. God makes it possible for us to do everything through Christ who gives us strength.

The more we realize these truths, the stronger and more confident we'll become.

Father, thank you for cherishing me the way you do. I confess that I can't always see myself the way you see me because my thinking gets distorted at times. I want to be strong, and that requires knowing truth and immersing myself in truth. Help me to remember that I am wonderful because you made me that way. I'm your workmanship. You value me far and above anything I can imagine. I am unique. I am loved. And thanks to you, I have a résumé that outshines anything this world has to offer. My status in you is worth bragging about. Would you get these truths into my heart and mind and help them to stay there?

POWER STATEMENT

I am strong. I know who I am, and I realize my value comes from God.

REFLECTION AND RESPONSE

How do you see yourself? What does God think of you?

22

Reject Negative Messages

Do not conform to the pattern of this world,
but be transformed by the renewing of your mind.

Romans 12:2

Υou'll never amount to anything." "You're ugly." "You're too fat." "You're too skinny." Chip, chip, chip.

"What makes you think you're qualified to do that?" "Why can't you be like everyone else?" Chip, chip, chip.

"Your writing (speaking, singing, dancing) is pitiful." Chip, chip, chip.

"You're a terrible friend (employee, mom, wife)." Chip, chip, chip.

"God can't use you because of your past." "God won't forgive something like that." Chip, chip, chip.

"What makes you think God cares about that?" "What makes you think God cares about you?" Chip, chip, chip.

"There's no hope for this world." "There's no hope for your circumstances." "There's no hope for you." Chip, chip, chip.

Negative messages come to us in many ways—through self-talk, naysayers in our lives, the enemy, and the media. The words have power. Once ingested, they chip away at our emotional, mental, relational, and physical strength. They lead to stinking thinking and wrong beliefs. They turn us away from truth and cause us to live the lies.

We need to stop them in their tracks. Immediately. We can't allow them to control us.

Consider these things:

- Negative self-talk prevents us from moving forward, from doing all God wants us to do, and from receiving all God wants us to receive. It keeps us from having a full and productive life. On top of that, when we belittle ourselves, we're daring to criticize God's creation.
- God doesn't condemn. He convicts. If we're listening to condemnation, we're paying attention to the wrong voice. Romans 8:1 says, "Therefore, there is now no condemnation for those who are in Christ Jesus."
- The devil is a big fat liar. He will do whatever he can to snatch away the passion, promise, and hope God has given us. John 10:10 says that his goal is to steal, kill, and destroy. But Jesus came to give us life to the full. We need to immerse ourselves in what Jesus says.

As these messages come to us and try to work their way into our spirits, we need to counter them with truth. For example, the lie that says God can't use us because of our past: We can reject that with, "My past is forgiven. God can use me in powerful ways to minister to people in similar situations today." We can refute "Why can't you be like everyone else?" with "I'm one of a kind. I'm incomparable."

To help us renew our minds and to further reinforce these

truths, we can write them on sticky notes and post them on mirrors, cupboards, windows, computer screens, refrigerators—wherever we'll see them. We can underline important truths in God's Word. We can flood our minds with truth and speak truth. The more it's spoken out loud, the more our hearts will believe it.

Rather than letting negative messages chip away at our strength, let's be fortified by what God has to say.

God, negative messages are everywhere, and they can zap my strength. If I'm not careful, I start believing the lies and go down the wrong path of stinking thinking. That's not good, nor is that honoring to you. In order to be the strong person you want me to be and to do the things you have planned for my life, I need to renew my mind. When I encounter negative messages, Lord, would you whisper your truths in my ear? Would you help me to discern what's true and what's not? Would you help me to reject any message that's not of you and to hear clearly the messages you want me to receive? Thank you that with your help I can be strong.

POWER STATEMENT

When confronted with negative messages, I will contradict them with truth. I will not allow them to chip away at my strength.

REFLECTION AND RESPONSE

What negative messages have you received? Write them down, and beside them write the truth. If you don't know the truth, ask God to reveal it to you.

23

Quit Playing the Comparison Game

*For we are His workmanship [His own master work, a work
of art], created in Christ Jesus [reborn from above—spiritually
transformed, renewed, ready to be used] for good works, which
God prepared [for us] beforehand [taking paths which He set],
so that we would walk in them [living the good life which He
prearranged and made ready for us].*

Ephesians 2:10 AMP

Linda brought several boxes filled with handmade pottery
to our meeting and gave each of us the opportunity to
choose one item as a gift. She had a wide variety of beautiful pieces—vases, plates, pots, and bowls—which made for a
tough decision. I gazed at the assortment and considered the
options, and then I discovered a pot I couldn't resist. It had
my name written all over it. Unlike any of the other pots, it
was full-bodied, lumpy, lopsided, and had a warped mouth. I
loved it.

My special acquisition now sits on a shelf in my living
room and serves as a visual reminder of how the Master Potter
created each of us differently. I share the characteristics of that
pot, and although I might seem peculiar, I'm a vessel God can
use mightily for his work.

I know that. I teach that. Yet sometimes I get distracted

by a person named Penelope Perfect. If I fall into her trap, she causes me to doubt who I am and leaves me in a state of discontentment.

You know Penelope, don't you? She ...

- is witty, charming, and wise;
- makes her own clothes, is a fabulous cook, and maintains a spotless house;
- has obedient, well-behaved children who excel in everything they do;
- leads a weekly international Bible study;
- publishes a new best-selling book every month;
- is an eloquent, hilarious, and dynamic communicator;
- runs a fortune 500 company and owns a private jet;
- established multiple charities around the world;
- plays fifteen musical instruments—some while standing on her head;
- has a flawless body with muscles and curves in all the right places;
- and when she enters a room, awe-inspiring music plays and heads slowly turn.

We can find Penelope on Facebook, in meetings, at church, and lots of other places, reminding us of how perfect she is and how much we lack. She's dangerous!

We might say, "Why can't I be more like her?" We might envy her life. But doing that is unproductive. It undermines our confidence and strength and causes us to question our purpose.

One day I had an aha moment while reading Psalm 139:16, which says, "All the days ordained for me were written in your book before one of them came to be." If I'm so set on being someone else and living their ordained days, who will do the things I was created to do with my ordained days? Who will tell the stories that only I can tell? Who will touch the lives that only I can touch?

No one can do me like I can do me. No one can do you like you can do you. God gave us our own ordained days to do things nobody else can do.

We're incomparable. Let's be strong in who we are.

Penelope Perfect is a dangerous person, Lord. When she distracts me, she causes me to forget who I am. She tempts me to be just like her. But you didn't create me to be like anyone else, Lord. I'm incomparable. And you have things for me to do that nobody else can do. Who will do them if I don't? You have a purpose and plan for me, and it's not Penelope Perfect's purpose and plan. Help me to be strong in who I am. I want to be the best me I can be, and I want to serve you in incomparable ways. Thank you for the one and only me!

POWER STATEMENT

I am incomparable. God gave me my own ordained days to do things nobody else can do.

REFLECTION AND RESPONSE

Do you ever have problems with Penelope Perfect? How does she make you feel? Why is playing the comparison game dangerous, and how does it affect your strength?

24

Keep Your Protection in Place

Finally, be strong in the Lord and in his mighty power.
Put on the full armor of God, so that you can take your stand
against the devil's schemes. For our struggle is not against flesh
and blood, but against the rulers, against the authorities, against
the powers of this dark world and against the spiritual forces of
evil in the heavenly realms. Therefore put on the full armor
of God, so that when the day of evil comes, you may be able to
stand your ground, and after you have done everything, to stand.

Ephesians 6:10–13

The group of Little-Leaguers huddled around Coach Chuck, who was giving them a refresher course on the fundamentals of baseball. After demonstrating the proper way to hold the bat and hit the ball, he asked, "Now, boys, what does it take to win games?"

My enthusiastic son's hand shot up immediately. "I know, I know!"

"Okay, Ryan, what does it take?"

"A cup."*

Not quite the response Coach expected. What he really wanted to hear was *runs*. Runs win games. But I couldn't help

---

*   If you're unfamiliar with the term, see definition #14 of "cup" at
    dictionary.com.

but be amazed at my son's brilliant answer—one that leads to an important truth: Players need protection. They can't be victorious if they're in the dirt, writhing in pain.

The apostle Paul understood this concept well, and in his letter to the Ephesians he gave them a pep talk about how important it was to draw their strength from the Lord and to be empowered through their union with him. He informed the Ephesians of their enemy's plans to defeat them and laid out the team strategy for how to stand their ground, remain strong, and overcome their adversary.

Paul emphasized that protection was vital to the outcome of the game. Because we face the same opposition, his counsel to the Ephesians is applicable for us.

First, we need to know what we're up against. We have an enemy with the goal of rendering us ineffective. He wants to weaken us. To deceive us. To tempt us. To destabilize us. To discourage us. To rob us of joy and peace and hope and life—abundant life. First Peter 5:8 says that our "enemy the devil prowls around like a roaring lion looking for someone to devour." It's imperative for us to know how to resist him and how to stand firm in our faith.

These are Paul's instructions from Ephesians 6:14–17: "Stand firm then, with the belt of truth buckled around your waist, with the breastplate of righteousness in place, and with your feet fitted with the readiness that comes from the gospel of peace. In addition to all this, take up the shield of faith, with which you can extinguish all the flaming arrows of the evil one. Take the helmet of salvation and the sword of the Spirit, which is the word of God."

The first thing Paul mentions is truth, our foundational

piece of protection. The enemy is a liar and an accuser. Because of that, we must know truth—the truth about God and the truth about ourselves. We must speak truth, practice truth, and, without wavering, stand in truth. We get truth from the Word of God—the sword of the Spirit—our indispensable weapon.

Paul closes his coaching session with a reminder to pray and stay alert.

If we follow his advice and keep our protection in place, it'll always be a winning season, no matter how hard the battle.

God, thank you for giving me everything I need to stand firm in my faith and to overcome the adversary. Thank you for my belt of truth and for your Word where I find truth. Thank you for the breastplate of righteousness that can guard my heart. Thank you for preparing my feet with the gospel of peace. Thank you for my shield that deflects the enemy's fiery arrows, and for the helmet of salvation that protects my mind. Best of all, thank you for my weapon, the sword of the Spirit. Help me to use it skillfully. I want to remind the enemy what a loser he is.

POWER STATEMENT

I will be strong in the Lord and in his mighty power. I have all I need to defeat the enemy and to remind him what a loser he is.

REFLECTION AND RESPONSE

Thank God for the protection he provides, and ask him to help you wield the sword of the Spirit skillfully. What does it take to do that?

25

Grow Deep Roots

*"But blessed are those who trust in the LORD and have
made the LORD their hope and confidence. They are like trees
planted along a riverbank, with roots that reach deep into the
water. Such trees are not bothered by the heat or worried
by long months of drought. Their leaves stay green,
and they never stop producing fruit."*

Jeremiah 17:7–8 NLT

One of the things I excel at is killing plants. Although I know what needs to be done (thanks to my horticulturist friend), I have trouble giving them proper attention. I forget to water them. I fail to feed them so they can grow healthy and strong. And I have no idea whether they should have sun or shade. In my care, they go from productive to pitiful in no time.

I was proud of myself for doing a pretty good job with Leonard, a plant I received while hospitalized, but after several months he started to look scraggly and sad. So I did something unusual for me—purchased a larger container and fresh soil, and took on the process of replanting him.

As I removed Leonard from his small pot and shook off the old dirt, I noticed that his roots were scrunched together in a tight ball. They had nowhere to go. And after I placed him in the bigger pot with fresh soil, I witnessed a change in his demeanor. He started to thrive. He had wiggled his roots around, and eventually they spread out and took hold. What a difference his deeper roots made!

Observing this process gave the Jeremiah verses above more meaning for me. They say that those who trust in the Lord and make him their hope and confidence are like trees with deep roots. Here are a few fun facts I've learned about roots:

- They are the lifeline for the tree.
- They feed, strengthen, and anchor the tree, keeping it straight and stable.
- They require water, nutrients, and oxygen, which come from the soil.
- They take nutrients out of the soil and use them to produce what they need for growth, development, and repair.
- They store extra food for future use.

Just as a tree depends on natural resources to survive, we need our spiritual resources.

Water: In John 7:37–38, Jesus said, "If anyone is thirsty, let him come to Me and drink! He who believes in Me [who adheres to, trusts in, and relies on Me], as the Scripture has said, 'From his innermost being will flow *continually* rivers of living water'" (AMP). (When Jesus mentioned rivers of living water, he was referring to the Holy Spirit.)

Nutrients: Colossians 3:16 says, "Let the word of Christ dwell in you richly" (ESV). And Jesus said in Matthew 4:4, "It is written: 'Man shall not live on bread alone, but on every word that comes from the mouth of God.'"

Oxygen: Acts 17:28 says, "For in him we live and move and

have our being." Like with oxygen, we can't see God, but we need him to exist.

Trusting in God—and putting our hope and confidence in him—makes us strong and fruitful. As we feed on his Word, store extra food for future use, and drink deeply of the Living Water, we'll be more anchored and ready to withstand the heat, droughts, and storms of life.

Lord, I want to be like the tree planted along the riverbank with roots that reach deep into the water. That way I won't be bothered by the heat and drought and stormy weather of life. I can be productive and strong, when I trust in you and make you my hope and confidence. Thank you for your Word that gives me nutrition, and thank you for the Living Water that I can drink of freely. Thank you for allowing me to live and move and have my being in you. You've given me all the resources I need to survive.

POWER STATEMENT

Because I trust in the Lord and have made him my hope and confidence, I will be strong and productive, like a tree with deep roots.

REFLECTION AND RESPONSE

How are your roots? Are they scrunched together in a tight ball or are they reaching deep? How can you make them stronger and healthier?

26

Rejoice in Problems and Trials

*We can rejoice, too, when we run into problems and trials,
for we know that they help us develop endurance. And endurance
develops strength of character, and character strengthens our
confident hope of salvation. And this hope will not lead to
disappointment. For we know how dearly God loves us, because
he has given us the Holy Spirit to fill our hearts with his love.*

Romans 5:3–5 NLT

Yay! Yippee! More problems. More trials. How exciting! Please,
please, please give me more, Lord. I want to develop endurance.
I want to develop strength of character.

Have you ever prayed like that? Me either. That would be
similar to praying for patience, which I learned many years ago
never to do again.

Yet Romans 5:3 tells us we should rejoice when we run into
trials. And James 1:2–4 says we should consider it pure joy, to
be happy, to regard it as a gift, when tests and challenges come
at us from all sides. How is that possible?

That's a difficult question to answer, but as I reflect on my
life and what God has brought me through, I can see how he
hasn't wasted anything. He's used the tough stuff to shape me
and mold me into the person he wants me to be. I am who I am
today because of God's unique grooming process.

I'm not going to lie and say the process has always been easy. It hasn't. But I know the outcome would have been entirely different if I had chosen to dwell in the depths of despair rather than to submit to God's plans and purposes and lift my heart and arms to him.

Here's what's happened: My faith has deepened. My heart has softened. My compassion for others has expanded. My endurance has increased. My perseverance has helped me stay the course. My appreciation for grace has grown exponentially. My love for God has filled my life. My knowledge of God's character has intensified. I've gained spiritual muscle, the confidence to trust in a big God, and the ability to stand firm through the storms of life.

I know people who haven't had the "blessing" of being challenged, and others who've chosen to ignore God's presence in their trials. They consider a broken fingernail a major life crisis.

The opposite scenarios remind me of the catchy advertising jingle for a popular garbage bag that says, "Hefty, Hefty, Hefty! Wimpy, wimpy, wimpy!" The commercials boast about the benefits of using their product. "When the pressure's on, Hefty bags stretch, while wimpy bags break."

I want to be the kind of person who stretches under pressure. I want to be a woman who can handle the piles of garbage life throws at her. Yes, I'd love to skip the hard stuff. And yes, I wish the way were plain and easy. But because I know it strengthens my character, and because it motivates me to lean into God and to know him better, I'll choose to rejoice. My hope will not disappoint.

Thank you, Lord, for helping me see how problems and trials benefit me. It's during the difficult times that my head knowledge of you has become heart knowledge. I've seen how you work, and I've experienced your presence in ways I wouldn't have otherwise. With an easy life I'd have no need for confidence in you. Thank you that I can always count on your grace when the going gets tough. It's what helps me endure. Lord, I want to have a hefty faith rather than a wimpy faith. If that means needing to go through your grooming process, I will acquiesce and rejoice.

POWER STATEMENT

I will rejoice in problems and trials because they help me develop endurance, strength of character, and confidence.

REFLECTION AND RESPONSE

What have you learned through problems and trials, and how have they strengthened your character?

27

Find Joy

May the God of hope fill you with all joy and peace
as you trust in him, so that you may overflow with hope
by the power of the Holy Spirit.

Romans 15:13

My brother Marvin and I were being silly and playing around with words one day many years ago, and we created a new term for a special kind of person: G'doozer. I hadn't thought about that for a long time, but it came to mind today.

Here's how I'd describe a G'doozer. Her countenance sparkles. She's pleasant to be around, full of life, overflows with hope, and displays amazing fortitude. She arouses curiosity. People wonder what makes her tick. A G'doozer is someone who exhibits joy—a person who oozes God. That's the kind of person I want to be.

Two of my favorite definitions for joy are "peace dancing" and "a smile inside." Another definition I've held onto is this one by Robert Schuller: "Joy is not the absence of suffering; it is the presence of God."* We wouldn't know joy without sorrow, pain, and trials. A couple of its benefits are that it causes healing (Proverbs 17:22) and gives strength (Nehemiah 8:10).

At times when my husband and I were going through difficult circumstances, people would ask questions like this: "How

---

* http://img.sermonindex.net/modules/articles/article_pdf.php?aid=30583.

do you do it? You've gone through so much, yet you always seem so strong and calm." The observers didn't realize they were seeing the fruit of our relationship with the Lord on display.

So let's answer the big questions: Where do we find this joy? How do we become a G'doozer?

According to the Bible, joy comes from doing the following:

Spending time in God's presence: "You will fill me with joy in your presence" (Psalm 16:11).

Trusting in God: "May the God of hope fill you with all joy and peace as you trust in him" (Romans 15:13).

Remaining in him: " 'I am the vine; you are the branches. If you remain in me and I in you, you will bear much fruit; apart from me you can do nothing' " (John 15:5). Galatians 5:22 says that joy is a "fruit of the Spirit."

Reading God's Word: "The precepts of the LORD are right, giving joy to the heart" (Psalm 19:8).

Obeying his commands: "If you keep my commands, you will remain in my love, just as I have kept my Father's commands and remain in his love. I have told you this so that my joy may be in you and that your joy may be complete" (John 15:10–11).

Watching him work: "For you make me glad by your deeds, LORD; I sing for joy at what your hands have done" (Psalm 92:4).

Keeping our hope alive: "Be joyful in hope" (Romans 12:12).

Joy is part of the abundant life Jesus said he came to give. It's possible to have even when life stinks. And when joy is present, it makes an impact. A big one.

God, what a wonderful gift joy is! It's good for my health, it gives strength, and it looks good on me. I love that the more time I spend with you and delighting in you, the more joy I have. And I love the feeling of having a smile inside even when life is tough. Thank you that joy is possible in the midst of heartache and suffering and trials. Paul and Silas exhibited joy after they were wrongly accused, beaten, and imprisoned, and people noticed. Because of their joy, the jailer, his family, and some of the prisoners came to know you. I want joy that people can see, Lord. I want to make an impact in other people's lives. I want to be a G'doozer.

POWER STATEMENT

Joy is possible in all circumstances. I will find joy in God, and it will be on full display.

REFLECTION AND RESPONSE

How's your joy factor? Is it on display and causing people to take notice? What can you do to increase the joy you have?

28

Wait on the Lord

*Do you not know? Have you not heard? The Everlasting God,
the LORD, the Creator of the ends of the earth does not become
tired or grow weary; there is no searching of His understanding.
He gives strength to the weary, and to him who has no might
He increases power. Even youths grow weary and tired, and
vigorous young men stumble badly, but those who wait for the
LORD [who expect, look for, and hope in Him] will gain new
strength and renew their power; they will lift up their wings [and
rise up close to God] like eagles [rising toward the sun]; they will
run and not become weary, they will walk and not grow tired.*

Isaiah 40:28–31 AMP

I'm not a big fan of waiting. Are you? I can get antsy just
waiting three minutes for a pot of coffee to brew. Sometimes
I'll push the process. Instead of letting the coffeemaker finish
its job, I'll pull out the carafe and quickly slide my mug in its
place to catch the dripping liquid. While my mug is catching
drips, I'll attempt to pour what coffee is already in the carafe
into it. Once the mug is full, I'll slip the carafe back in its
place. Yes, I get my coffee, but I usually end up making a huge
mess in the meantime. If I had only waited, I would have saved
myself a lot of trouble. Impatience is definitely not a virtue.

Waiting may be inconvenient for us, and sometimes
it seems unbearable, but it can have a positive outcome.
Especially when we wait for the Lord. According to Isaiah,

those who wait for the Lord will gain new strength and renew their power. That's good, because life has a way of zapping us.

One important thing to note is that when we wait for the Lord, we need to let him do his job, not take matters into our own hands, as I do getting my coffee in the mornings. If we don't allow God to work out his plans and on his schedule, we'll make a mess of things and won't receive the full benefits of what he has in store for us.

God is more concerned about who he wants us to become rather than our immediate comfort. It's in the waiting period that he shapes us and develops our spiritual muscle. While we wait, God teaches us about his attributes and his power. He invites us to know him better. We learn how to trust and why we can trust. And in the process of that, we gain strength of character and a more durable faith.

If we keep our attention on God during the waiting (and not on our circumstances), we grasp valuable truths. Here are a few I've added to my mental storehouse, and they've helped me endure some of my hardest days:

He will never abandon me. His arms are long. He answers prayer. His grace is sufficient. He knows me better than I know myself. He knows just what I need. He's my provider. He loves me more than anything I can imagine. He's creative. He's never in a hurry, but he's always right on time. Nothing is too big for him to accomplish. Nothing is too small for his attention. His name is I AM. (He is who he says he is.) He keeps his promises. He never changes.

For me, the benefits of waiting for God far outweigh the inconvenience. The best perk is that he waits with us. That alone makes waiting worthwhile.

God, I don't enjoy waiting, but it's worthwhile when I wait on you. Thank you for waiting with me. Thank you for the hope you give as I wait. Thank you for the spiritual strength you develop within me as I trust in you. Thank you for teaching me who you are within the waiting process. Thank you for the valuable truths you've given me to hold onto when trials come. Thank you for being more concerned about who you want me to be than about my comfort or convenience. I'm not always excited about your process of developing strength, Lord, but I've learned that your understanding is not the same as mine and your ways are good ways. For that I give you praise.

POWER STATEMENT

When I wait for God and keep my attention on him, I gain spiritual muscle and learn valuable truths.

REFLECTION AND RESPONSE

When have you had to wait on God? How did you handle it? What did you learn in the waiting process?

29
Store Up Reserves

My health may fail, and my spirit may grow weak,
but God remains the strength of my heart; he is mine forever.
Psalm 73:26 NLT

When my friend Ann was in her last hours on earth, I felt an urge to visit her in the hospital. She had poured into my life in many ways as a mentor, friend, teacher, and role model, and I couldn't bear the thought of her dying without my telling her how grateful I was.

I walked into the room and stood at the end of her bed. The woman I saw was frail, her teeth decayed because of the medicines used to prolong her life. She wasn't at all like the strong person she was before cancer ravaged her body.

Before I could speak one word, Ann said in a perky voice, "Oh Twila, how good it is to see you. I've been praying for you." Although her health had failed and her spirit had grown weak, she exhibited strength of heart, joy, and peace—a beautiful representation of the words in Psalm 73:26.

As I reflect on Ann now, I think about my own recent experience with chemotherapy treatments. Some days were hard. Really hard. During that time, I wrote this on my Care Pages site: "My brain is tired. My eyeballs are tired. My fingers and toes are tired. My body is tired. And sometimes I wonder how much longer I can make it. But I continue to trust God. He remains the strength of my heart. He is mine forever."

He remains the strength of my heart. My spirit knows what that means, but trying to explain it is not so easy. How does God remain the strength of a person's heart?

My thought process took me in a lot of directions, and I finally landed on something that makes sense to me. It's the result of storing up reserves. Just as …

- Joseph stored up grain to get the Egyptians through the years of famine (see Genesis);
- roots of plants and trees store up food to get through the winter; and
- reservoirs store water to use for emergencies.

In a similar way, we can store up spiritual reserves. When the hard times come—or when our health fails and our spirit grows weak—the resources are there for us. What we know about God remains. He's the strength of our heart. Our rock.

Here's how it works. The more we trust God, the more knowledge we have of who he is and what he's able to do. We tuck that away in our minds and hearts for when the next challenge comes. The more we read God's Word and fill our minds with truth, the more those words dwell within us and are available to bring comfort, encouragement, and reminders of God's power. The more trials we face, the more endurance, strength of character, and hope we store up. The more we allow the Holy Spirit to work in our lives, the more spiritual fruit we have on supply.

As we draw on those reserves, people will notice, and God will get the glory.

Lord, I praise you for being the strength of my heart. You're my rock, my joy, my heartbeat. Thank you for your Word that brings comfort, encouragement, and reminders of your power. Thank you for helping me to know you better through the times I've trusted you. Thank you for the fruit that's produced because of the Holy Spirit at work in my life. Thank you for the endurance, strength of character, and hope I have. Thank you for the many spiritual resources you've given me to draw upon for when the hard times come or when my health may fail. Lord, I want people to see that you are my strength through all I face. May my life shine the light on you.

POWER STATEMENT

I want God to remain the strength of my heart; therefore, I will store up spiritual resources today.

REFLECTION AND RESPONSE

What do the words in Psalm 73:26 mean to you?

30

Accept Help and Support from Others

So Joshua did as Moses said, and fought with Amalek; and Moses, Aaron, and Hur went up to the hilltop. Now when Moses held up his hand, Israel prevailed, and when he lowered his hand [due to fatigue], Amalek prevailed. But Moses' hands were heavy and he grew tired. So they took a stone and put it under him, and he sat on it. Then Aaron and Hur held up his hands, one on one side and one on the other side; so it was that his hands were steady until the sun set. So Joshua overwhelmed and defeated Amalek and his people with the edge of the sword.

Exodus 17:10–13 AMP

I have a confession: I'm not perfect. Hard to believe, isn't it? What I've written below is humbling, but I'm laying it out for the world to see.

My responsibilities include working long hours at home to provide an income for my family, caregiving for my husband, handling my son's ongoing issues, doing all the shopping and heavy lifting, cooking, coordinating multiple medical appointments, wrestling with never-ending paperwork, making important life decisions, managing my own health needs (when I can fit that in), attempting to keep the world spinning, and … and … and … The truth is I can't do it all. I get weary.

At times I struggle just to hold my head on my neck, yet I'm embarrassed when visitors see my clutter and the piles of unwashed pots and pans on the counter. I don't want them to know the real me—someone who has shortcomings. I'll admit I occasionally have trouble letting people into my life because of a crazy feeling that I'm being judged for what I haven't done.

Yes, I know that's flawed thinking—thinking I'm overcoming after years of trials and having no recourse but to rely on other people's help. I'm finally grasping this reality: I can't survive without support and assistance.

Even Moses couldn't. When Joshua fought Amalek, Moses stood at the top of the hill with his hands raised in prayer. While they were lifted high, the Israelites prevailed. But when Moses struggled and his arms dropped due to fatigue, the enemy overpowered them. Aaron and Hur brought a stone and encouraged Moses to sit, and they stood by his side to uphold him until the sun went down. Because of their support, the battle Moses oversaw was won.

Likewise, we can endure our battles with the help of others.

On many occasions friends, family, and church members have come alongside to keep me from falling. I had emergency gall bladder surgery that required a seven-day hospital stay three weeks after my daughter was born. I wasn't able to carry her for seven weeks. I also had a twenty-month-old son at home. It would have been an impossible situation without help.

After our run-in with the drunk driver, friends and acquaintances filled in at our Christian bookstore and vending company. They did chores, kid duty, ran errands, and watched over me.

During agonizing times with my husband's health issues and hospitalizations, my friend Jennifer mothered me, and my friend Nancy cared for our three children.

Most recently with my cancer treatments, numerous people have sustained our family through monetary gifts, meals, yard work, house projects, prayers, and encouragement.

Does accepting help mean that I'm weak? That Moses was weak? That you're weak? No. It means God provides what we need to keep us strong. It's a message worth remembering.

Loving God, thank you for the support and help of caring people. If I had to face my battles alone, I don't know how I would endure. Thank you for knowing who I need and what I need and right when I need it. You are so good to me. I like to think that I can do it all, and I get frustrated when I can't, but the reality is that nobody can. You created us for friendship and fellowship and to uphold each other. Even Moses became fatigued and needed help. Thank you for reminding me that accepting assistance doesn't mean I'm weak. It means you love me enough to keep me strong through others.

POWER STATEMENT

God keeps me strong through the help of others. I will gratefully accept their support.

REFLECTION AND RESPONSE

How are you at accepting assistance from others? What battles have you faced that you couldn't have survived without the help of other people? How did it make you feel to have their support? Is there someone who might need your help today?

PART FOUR

The Power to Be Courageous

Courage will follow when faith takes the lead.
(Author Unknown)

31

Practice Courage Every Day

Be strong, and let your heart take courage,
all you who wait for the LORD!
Psalm 31:24 ESV

A tightrope is stretched across Niagara Falls, and a performer asks a member in the audience if she thinks he can make it across the rope without plunging into the raging waters below. "Absolutely," she says. "You have a great track record, and you've never had a problem with it before. I have no doubt that you can safely cross the tightrope."

After the tightrope walker successfully accomplishes his feat, he stands in front of the audience with a wheelbarrow. He asks a different woman, "Do you believe I can push this wheelbarrow across the tightrope without slipping and falling to my death?"

"Yes," she says. "I know you. You've done it many times without fail. You're a professional, and I'm confident in your ability."

"Okay, get in," he says.

All of a sudden the story changes. Now the woman isn't so sure. She had said she believed in the performer's abilities, but she wasn't willing to trust her life in his hands.

Sound familiar? We might say we believe God is able. We might say God can do anything. We might say he has a great track record. But are we willing to put our life, our health, our hopes, our dreams, our future, our family, our finances—everything—into his hands? Are we willing to put it all on the line and get into the wheelbarrow with him?

That's what trust is, and trust involves risk. We surrender our own control to someone else. And it can be scary at times. It's not easy to stay in the wheelbarrow when the tightrope starts shaking. But we need to remember that God's hand is steady, and he is worthy of our trust.

Shortly after I received the diagnosis of breast cancer, a friend sent me a colorful wood sign with four words on it. *Practice courage every day.* As I pondered the meaning, I realized that courage implies confidence, and confidence (or trust) in God is the quality of mind or spirit that enables me to face unknowns, difficulties, danger, pain, and whatever else comes my way without fear.

My idea of courage is to live like I believe God is who he says he is and will do what he says he will do.

For me, to practice courage every day means to practice trusting God every day. The more I trust God, the more I know God. The more I know God, the more comfortable the wheelbarrow becomes.

Almighty God, I know you. I know your track record. I've seen you accomplish great things and perform wonders. You are a God who never fails, a God who is faithful, and a God in whose ability I'm confident. Yet when I'm asked to hop in the wheelbarrow and to trust you with my health, my family, my finances, my dreams, my future, and everything else in my life, that's when it gets personal. Would you help me have the courage to take the risk and to be confident in your steady hands? I want to practice courage every day, and that means trusting you.

POWER STATEMENT

I will live like I believe God is who he says he is and will do what he says he will do.

REFLECTION AND RESPONSE

Is there an area in your life where God is saying, "Trust me, Child. Get in the wheelbarrow with me"? What is it? How are you doing with that?

32

Get Your Eyes off Yourself

But Moses said to God,
"Who am I that I should go to Pharaoh and bring the Israelites
out of Egypt?" And God said, "I will be with you."

Exodus 3:11–12

The story in Exodus 3 and 4 is fascinating. Moses, tending his sheep in the desert, sees a burning bush, but the bush isn't consumed. He goes closer to check it out and hears a voice. "Moses! Moses!" It's God. Realizing he's standing on holy ground, Moses removes his sandals.

Then God reveals his great plan: "I've seen the misery of the Israelites. I've heard them crying because of their slave drivers, and I'm concerned about their suffering. It's time to rescue them from the hands of the Egyptians and lead them to a land flowing with milk and honey. Good news, Moses! I've chosen you to make this happen."

If Moses hadn't been barefoot, he'd be shaking in his boots. "Wait a minute, God. You're sending *me*? Who am I to do a job like that? I'm just a grownup basket case. I can't do it. Can't you ple-e-e-e-a-se send someone else?"

God's response? "I will be with you. It doesn't matter who you are, Moses. It matters who I am."

Once Moses took his eyes off himself, he accomplished amazing things for God.

I've had many "Moses moments" in my life. When asked years ago to play piano for Bible Study Fellowship, I questioned why God didn't choose a better musician to do it. "I'm a scriptural pianist, Lord. My left hand doesn't know what my right hand is doing." God reminded me that he didn't call someone else; he called me.

When God made it clear he wanted me to write, I said, "Lord, how am I supposed to write? I can't even talk without problems." God reminded me to trust him.

When God wanted me to become a speaker, I protested. "But Lord, don't you remember the excuse I gave for not writing? You know how I get tongue-tied." God reminded me of the time he used a donkey to get his message across.

Each time I've feared my inadequacies, my underlying thought process was: "What if I fail or look like a fool?" And God reminds me that it's not about me; it's about him. If it's about him and for him and by him, doesn't it just make sense that he will help me do his work?

God doesn't need our help. He can get the job done with us or without us, but he chooses us to carry out particular works so we might be blessed and bless others. We can take courage in the fact that God never gives us a job without equipping us for it. He doesn't want our competence. He wants our obedience. And if we walk forward, hand in hand with him, he will come through for us every time. Guaranteed.

God, I have big problems when my eyes are on myself instead of on you. I see my insecurities, my weaknesses, and my shortcomings, and I forget that it doesn't matter who I am. It matters who you are. You don't want my competence, and you certainly don't want my excuses. You want my willingness to do what you ask. So rather than questioning, "Who am I?" like Moses did, would you help me to say, "Look who God is"? Lord, I want to accomplish big things for you. The only way for me to do that is to step out in obedience and to trust you for the results.

POWER STATEMENT

When God asks me to do something, I will say yes, even if it's scary. Who I am doesn't matter. Who God is, does.

REFLECTION AND RESPONSE

Has God ever asked you to do a particular task that was scary, or that you didn't feel competent to do? What was it? How did you answer God and how did it work out? What is he calling you to do right now?

33

Cling to God's Promises

So we see that they were not able to enter [into His rest—
the promised land] because of unbelief and an
unwillingness to trust in God.

Hebrews 3:19 AMP

God is a promise keeper, but when circumstances appear contrary to what he's said, our faith sometimes falters. Rather than clinging to his promises and moving forward in trust, we choose to live by sight.

That's what happened with the Israelites in Numbers 13–14. God gave Moses these instructions: "Send out men to explore the land of Canaan, the land I am giving to the Israelites. Send one leader from each of the twelve ancestral tribes" (Numbers 13:2 NLT). Did you notice the promise?

The appointed men scouted the bountiful land, experienced the fabulous fruit, and at the end of forty days returned with their reports. "The land does flow with milk and honey! The fruit is amazing. Look how big it is!" And then the tone changed.

Ten of the spies had this to say:

"BUT the people there are powerful. The cities are fortified and very large."

"BUT we can't attack them. They're stronger than we are."

"BUT there are giants in the land."

"BUT we seemed like grasshoppers compared to them."

"IF ONLY we had died in Egypt or in the desert."

"WHY is the Lord doing this to us? We're going to die by the sword. Our wives and kids will be taken as plunder."

"Wouldn't it be better for us to go back to Egypt?"

However, two of the spies—Caleb and Joshua—had a different perspective:

"We should go up and take possession of the land, for we can certainly do it" (Numbers 13:30).

"The land we passed through and explored is exceedingly good. If the Lord is pleased with us, he will lead us into that land, a land flowing with milk and honey, and will give it to us. Only do not rebel against the Lord. And do not be afraid of the people of the land, because we will devour them. Their protection is gone, but the Lord is with us. Do not be afraid of them" (Numbers 14:7–9).

The ten let their fear consume them. They were full of excuses and if-onlys, and their distorted thinking left them teeming with imaginative story lines. In spite of the many signs God had performed among them, they refused to trust him. By rejecting his promises, they were, in a sense, saying they knew better than God what was best for them. God wasn't pleased, and instead of entering their promised land, the ten disbelieving leaders—and millions of followers—wandered aimlessly in the desert until they died.

On the other hand, Joshua and Caleb clung to God's promises, even though they seemed impossible. And even though they were surrounded by naysayers. Because they had confidence in God's ability, he honored their courage. The land of milk and honey became their home forty years later.

Likewise, if we trust God to keep his word, God will bless us with his best for our lives.

God, I praise you for being a promise keeper. You are always true to your word. I don't want anything holding me back from receiving your best for my life. Not excuses. Not fears. Not if-onlys. Not what-ifs. Not naysayers. Not disbelief. Not grumbling. I want to be like Joshua and Caleb who believed what you said and trusted your ability to accomplish your plan. Help me to be courageous and to keep my eyes on you. Help me to continue to trust you and cling to your promises even when my circumstances look contrary to what you've said. You will honor me when I live by faith and not by sight.

POWER STATEMENT

I will remember that God is a promise keeper, and I'll cling to his promises regardless of how things appear.

REFLECTION AND RESPONSE

What are some of the promises God has given you? What's holding you back from believing them?

34

Be Mindful of His Presence

*"Have I not commanded you? Be strong and courageous.
Do not be afraid; do not be discouraged, for the LORD
your God will be with you wherever you go."*

Joshua 1:9

Consider Joshua's circumstances at the time he was given the words above. He had just inherited Moses' job of leading the Israelites—more than six hundred thousand men, plus women and children—and it was time for them to cross the Jordan River. Not only did he have the enormous responsibility of getting millions of people and their animals and belongings safely to the other side, but he had the added burden of doing it while the river was at flood stage.

He was well aware that once they got through that huge trial, they'd encounter corrupt and brutal nations that were greater and stronger than them, with large cities that had walls up to the sky. They'd face giants and countless unknowns.

Yet he was told again and again, "Be strong. Be courageous. Don't be terrified. Don't be discouraged."

If someone came to us while we were up against one of the biggest challenges of our life, and spewed out the same instructions, we might feel like slapping them upside the head (in

Christian love, of course). We have enough people in our lives spouting advice without offering any physical help.

But in Joshua's case, God was the one giving the orders, and he wasn't just throwing out words. He was telling him, "Hey, Joshua, you *can* be strong and courageous. I'm here right now, and I will accompany you on your journey. I'm not going to leave your side. Remember who I am. Remember what I can do and what I plan to do. Remember my promise that awaits you."

God didn't expect Joshua to muster up strength and courage on his own. God doesn't expect us to do that either.

Throughout Scripture we have multiple reminders that God is with us and will be with us. He wants us to internalize those truths. If we have a conscious awareness that he is escorting us as we face unknowns, battles, giants, unfamiliar territories, tests, danger, or other situations that cause us to tremble, we'll be better able to charge ahead fearlessly.

We have no reason to be terrified or discouraged, for the Lord our God is with us wherever we go.

Let the following verses serve as a reminder of that important truth:

- "So do not fear, for I am with you; do not be dismayed, for I am your God." (Isaiah 41:10)
- "When you pass through the waters, I will be with you." (Isaiah 43:2)
- Even though I walk through the darkest valley, I will fear no evil, for you are with me. (Psalm 23:4)
- I have set the LORD always before me; because he is at my right hand, I shall not be shaken. (Psalm 16:8 ESV)

- "So be strong and courageous! Do not be afraid and do not panic before them. For the LORD your God will personally go ahead of you. He will neither fail you nor abandon you." (Deuteronomy 31:6 NLT)

Lord, I see a recurring message throughout Scripture. You promised your people again and again that you would be with them. That you would never fail or abandon them. In the same way, you've given me assurances of your presence wherever I go. And because you're with me, I don't have cause to be afraid. But, Lord, sometimes it's hard for me to remember because I can't see you in the flesh. Would you keep me mindful of your presence and continue to send me frequent reminders? When I'm aware of you, I can be strong and courageous.

POWER STATEMENT

Because God is with me, I can be strong and courageous. I have no reason to be afraid.

REFLECTION AND RESPONSE

What does it mean to you when God says, "I am with you"? How does knowing God is with you give you courage? As a side project, start making a list of all the times you see promises of his presence in the Bible.

35

Consider the Size of Your God

*David said to the Philistine, "You come against me with sword
and spear and javelin, but I come against you in the name of the
LORD Almighty, the God of the armies of Israel, whom you
have defied. This day the LORD will deliver you into my hands
… and the whole world will know that there is a God in Israel.
All those gathered here will know that it is not by sword or
spear that the LORD saves; for the battle is the LORD'S,
and he will give all of you into our hands."*

1 Samuel 17:45–47

Giants charge into our lives making a boisterous statement
that they're insurmountable. They taunt us relentlessly,
haunt us in our sleep, and remind us of how small and helpless
we are. While not all of them are made of flesh and blood, we
can gain some helpful insights on how to conquer them from
the verses in 1 Samuel 17.

Most of us are familiar with the Philistine named Goliath.
He stood taller than nine feet, and his armor and weapons alone
weighed more than many of the Israelite soldiers. Whenever he
emerged to bellow his menacing statements, dismay and terror
filled King Saul and his fighting men.

One day David arrived at the army camp to make a deliv-
ery for his dad and heard Goliath shout his usual contempt.

The words offended him, and he asked, "How dare he defy the armies of the living God?" So David, a mere teenager, volunteered to take on the massive man. After refusing the bulky armor Saul offered, he advanced with a shepherd's staff, a sling, and a stone.

As David approached the Philistine, Goliath (with his shield bearer in front of him) moved closer and closer. He bullied David. Cursed him. Mocked him. Threatened him. Tried to instill fear. But David didn't cower. Instead, he ran quickly toward the battle line to meet his imposing challenger head-on.

With boldness, David countered the hulk's bluster. "You've got some pretty fancy armor and weapons there, mister. And you have a nice compliant helper carrying your big shield. You act like you're hot stuff, and you talk a pretty good game. But I have something above and beyond all that. I have the unmatched power of the living God at work on my behalf. You might be intimidating and pretend to be superior to me, but you don't even begin to compare to my immeasurable God."

The rest of the account is well known. An unprotected kid, wielding a smooth stone from his sling, effortlessly toppled the Israelites' formidable opponent.

How could David stand up against the Philistine champion, when the entire Israelite army fled in terror each time he appeared? It boils down to this: David looked beyond the size of the giant and saw the size of his God. His faith was greater than his fear. The others bolted because they lived by sight.

From David's story, we can learn some important steps to overcoming giants:

- Whatever your giant's name, acknowledge it. Don't retreat in fear. Fear paralyzes.
- Realize that giants will invade your territory if they're not contested.
- Align your thinking with the enormity of your God, and turn your focus from the giant to him.
- Remember that the battle is God's. Put your trust in him rather than armor or weapons or self.
- Address your giant confidently with what you know to be true about the living God.
- Courageously press on with victory in mind.

Lord Almighty, I'm grateful that you're my God. You're a big God—bigger than any giants I'll ever face. Thank you that I don't need to be outfitted with the fanciest armor. I don't need a shield bearer. I don't need an illustrious education, the newest technology, highly trained reinforcements, or a thousand-page giant-killer manual. I just need to take courage in what I know to be true about you. Your power is unmatched, and I have your promise that you will do the fighting for me. When I look beyond the size of my giants and see the size of my God, I can walk forward in confidence and win the victory every time.

POWER STATEMENT

I have the unmatched power of the living God at work on my behalf. I will look beyond the size of my giants and see the size of my God.

REFLECTION AND RESPONSE

Are you facing any giants right now? What are they? What do you know to be true about your God?

36

Trust and Obey, Then Get out of the Way

God blesses those who obey him;
happy the man who puts his trust in the Lord.
Proverbs 16:20 TLB

Sometimes God asks us to do crazy, scary things. While he hasn't called me to build an ark or to lead a country, he's challenged me over the years with some pretty intimidating requests.

I was on the faculty of a writers conference and had arrived at my hotel just in time to freshen up before the pre-event meet-and-greet with other faculty members and conferees. The heavily promoted keynote speaker that year was the fabulous Chonda Pierce, an especially popular stand-up comedian. I had big plans to become best friends with her.

As I ironed my clothes, the phone rang. I picked it up, said hello, and the pleasant voice on the other end began talking. "Hi, Twila. This is Barbara Wells. I'm the director of the conference. We haven't met, and I don't know much about you, but we need your help. Chonda had to cancel because of a family emergency. We'd like you to do the three keynotes." She went on to tell me that the first one would be the next morning. "Oh, and by the way, we've invited the community to tomorrow night's session."

136

I listened to Barbara, but had a side conversation going with God at the same time. "You want me to do what, Lord? Are you kidding me? Do you know who Chonda Pierce is? Do you know that everyone coming to the conference is expecting her? You know it's impossible to fill her shoes, don't you?"

Then Barbara said, "I'm confident you can do it. I've been to your website."

After a few seconds in stunned silence, I asked, "Can I pray about it?"

"How long?"

Very funny, Lord.

She continued, "When I asked God what we should do, I heard a voice in my spirit that said, 'Twila Belk is here.'"

At that point she had me—I knew it was a God thing—so I told her I'd do it, but she had to promise prayer covering. Minutes after that conversation, I went to the meet-and-greet. I couldn't tell anyone about the new development. They'd all find out the next morning when I was introduced as Chonda's substitute.

Wow. Just wow.

What did I do? I called home and asked my husband to send an urgent request down our church's prayer chain. I paced and prayed and prayed and paced. I rehearsed the many sermons I give to others, reminded myself of God's bigness, and remembered his track record in my life.

Then I showed up the next morning with less than two hours sleep, stood on that stage, and delivered the first keynote. My mouth moved. God's message came out. And nobody booed. In fact, the audience gave God a standing ovation at the end. I survived, and God assured me that he knew what he was doing. Now, five years later, I've been asked to return to the conference as the publicized keynoter.

It's amazing what God can do when we trust and obey, then get out of the way.

Lord, as I think about the crazy things you ask me to do, I can't help but smile because I've seen how you work. The things you ask usually aren't normal or easy, and most of the time they're scary. They challenge me to trust you. But that's what it's all about, isn't it, Lord? You want to keep reinforcing who you are and how big you are. You want to keep reminding me that anything you call me to do will have your equipping, power, and presence involved. Thank you for teaching me that when I trust and obey, then get out of the way, you always show up and show off. May you receive all honor, glory, and praise.

POWER STATEMENT

When I trust and obey, then get out of the way, God will show up and show off.

REFLECTION AND RESPONSE

Has God ever given you a crazy, scary assignment? What was it? How did you respond? What did you learn about God at that time, and how does it encourage you to trust him more today?

37

Let God Guide You

I will lead the blind on roads they have never known;
I will guide them on paths they have never traveled.
Their road is dark and rough, but I will give light
to keep them from stumbling.
This is my solemn promise.

Isaiah 42:16 CEV

My young son Ryan joined me as I ran errands one day many years ago. Our first stop was the bank, and I steered the car into the drive-through lane behind a beige Mercedes Benz. A fancy dog with long, flowing blond hair held its head out the back window and happily observed the surrounding activity. I had seen the same car and dog while driving around town earlier in the week.

With curiosity aroused, I turned to Ryan. "What's up with that dog?"

"Well, Mom, maybe it's a seeing-eye dog," he said.

That's it! Why hadn't I thought of that before? The driver is blind! A crazy scenario filled my mind: The dog barks once if the traffic light is red. It barks twice if the light turns green. And it howls if there's a pothole to avoid.

Silly as it is, the mental picture reminded me that we have a seeing-eye God who promises to lead the blind by ways they have not known. He promises to guide them on never-traveled paths. And that's good news for us because we often face situations that make us feel like that blind driver. It could be a life-altering decision. A transition into new territory. Serious health challenges. A different job. The birth of a baby. The death of a close family member or friend. Divorce. The mission field. Anything that takes us into a strange environment.

When thrown into the unfamiliar, we don't know what obstacles or surprises or dangers lie ahead. Our creative imaginations might leave us wandering in the what-ifs. Fears and uncertainties might try to paralyze us.

But God offers encouragement in many ways.

Light through his Word: David said in Psalm 119:105, "Your word is a lamp for my feet, a light on my path."

His presence: "So do not fear, for I am with you" (Isaiah 41:10).

Prayer: Knowing that God listens, cares, and is trustworthy gives confidence and hope. I frequently use David's words from Psalm 25:4–5 as I pray: "Show me your ways, Lord, teach me your paths. Guide me in your truth and teach me, for you are God my Savior, and my hope is in you all day long."

His Spirit: The Holy Spirit plays many roles in our lives, including guide, helper, advocate, comforter, and counselor.

Wisdom, discernment, and revelation: God will give it, if we ask.

Timing: God often uses the timing of circumstances and words of others to guide and direct us.

Promises: One of many is found in Proverbs 3:5–6. If we trust him with all our hearts and acknowledge him in all our ways, he will direct our paths.

Peace: When we're at peace in our spirit, we can move forward in confidence.

God's help makes it possible for us to be courageous in our next steps.

Lord, so much of my life is unknown. I don't know what tomorrow holds or even what the rest of today holds. Yet I know you, and that's enough. You've promised to lead me and guide me. You've promised light to keep me from stumbling. You've promised to hold my hand and to never leave my side. I take great comfort in that, Lord. I'm grateful for your reassurance that my unfamiliar paths are not unfamiliar to you. You know the way, and I can trust you to make the rough places smooth. I praise you for being my seeing-eye God.

POWER STATEMENT

God will lead me on unknown roads and guide me on unfamiliar paths. I can trust him to turn my darkness to light and make the rough places smooth.

REFLECTION AND RESPONSE

What are ways God has led you and guided you in your past? How did you know when you were on the right path? What unknowns are you facing today, and how does Isaiah 42:16 encourage you?

38

Resolve to Inquire of the Lord

*Alarmed, Jehoshaphat resolved to inquire of the LORD,
and he proclaimed a fast for all Judah.*

2 Chronicles 20:3

Second Chronicles 20 tells us King Jehoshaphat received news that a vast army, intent on war, was rapidly approaching. He had good reason to believe he and his countrymen would be annihilated. Yes, Jehoshaphat was afraid. Who wouldn't be?

At that moment, he had a choice. He could:

- let his fear consume him;
- run away and let someone else deal with the problem;
- go into denial;
- eat five pounds of chocolate;
- or pause, put things in perspective, and press forward with purpose and promise.

Jehoshaphat knew where to go for help, as did the psalmist in Psalm 121:1–2, who said, "I lift up my eyes to the mountains—where does my help come from? My help comes from the LORD, the Maker of heaven and earth," and he resolved to inquire of the Lord. The NASB translation of 2 Chronicles 20:3 says that Jehoshaphat "turned his attention to seek the LORD."

Of course the encroaching enemy had his attention. But to keep his focus there would cause emotional and mental torment, and that would be as bad as the physical torture coming his way. He determined to put his fear aside and directed his thoughts toward God.

The people of Judah gathered at the temple, and standing before them Jehoshaphat rehearsed these truths about God in prayer: (1) He's the God who is in heaven. (2) He rules over all the kingdoms of the nations. (3) Power and might are in his hands. (4) No one can withstand him.

Jehoshaphat also declared that if calamity came upon them, they would stand in God's presence and cry out, and God would hear and save them.

He presented the problem to God and ended with this admission: "For we have no power to face this vast army that is attacking us. We do not know what to do, but our eyes are on you" (2 Chronicles 20:12).

Jehoshaphat took a risk and put his trust in God. He was willing to do that because his life and the lives of his countrymen depended on it. And the rest of 2 Chronicles 20 shows us how his faith in action resulted in victory. (We'll discuss this more in the next chapter, "Execute God's Battle Plan.")

Circumstances beyond our control can seem like battles to us, and fear and desperation are natural human responses. But what we do with those feelings and how we allow them to evolve will determine the outcome of our situation. Our best choice is to follow Jehoshaphat's example and (1) seek the Lord, (2) remind ourselves of truth, (3) acknowledge that we are powerless on our own, (4) admit that we don't have the answers, and (5) look to God for our courage and help.

So many times I've felt powerless to face my battles, Lord. And so many times I've asked the question, "What do I do when I don't know what to do?" Then I remember to lift my eyes and heart to you. You are the Maker of heaven and earth, and my help comes from you. You are the God who is in heaven. You rule over all the earth and everything in it. Power and might are in your hands. When I turn my attention to you in the midst of circumstances beyond my control, I'll see what you're able to do.

POWER STATEMENT

When circumstances are beyond my control and I don't know what to do, I will resolve to inquire of the Lord.

REFLECTION AND RESPONSE

Are you facing any battles, or do you have any circumstances in your life right now that are beyond your control? Anything that causes you to say, "I don't know what to do"? Take the time to write out a conversation with God, and say, "Lord, I don't know what to do about _____, but my eyes are on you." Give your list to him and watch him work.

39

Execute God's Battle Plan

He said: "Listen, King Jehoshaphat and all who live
in Judah and Jerusalem! This is what the LORD says to you:
'Do not be afraid or discouraged because of this vast army.
For the battle is not yours, but God's.'"

2 Chronicles 20:15

Jehoshaphat admitted that he and the people of Judah had no power to face the vast army that was attacking them. After he prayed, "We do not know what to do, but our eyes are on you," God sent them an important message through Jahaziel, a Levite:

- Don't be afraid. Don't be discouraged.
- You don't have to fight the battle. It isn't yours; it's God's.
- Take up your positions, stand firm, and see the deliverance God will give you.
- Go out and face them, and the Lord will be with you. (2 Chronicles 20:14–17)

Messages similar to these appear repeatedly in Scripture. Obviously, God wants to drive home a point.

The people of Judah took God at his word and bowed in worship, and some of the Levites stood up and praised the

Lord loudly. The next morning, as they headed out to face their attackers, Jehoshaphat gave them a hearty pep talk. He reminded them to have faith in the Lord and said that God would uphold them and give them success. He then appointed some of the men to sing to the Lord and praise him as they went out at the head of the army.

And this is my favorite part: 2 Chronicles 20:22 says, "As they began to sing and praise, the LORD set ambushes against the men of Ammon and Moab and Mount Seir who were invading Judah, and they were defeated."

Did you catch that? They sang their fight song—praise— and God did what he said he would do.

Here are a couple of significant things to note. (1) Praise is powerful. It silences the enemy and wins battles. (2) God is creative. He can do things in ways beyond our imagination. We need to remember that when we're in the midst of impossible-looking circumstances.

I like to think of this story in 2 Chronicles 20 as God's battle plan for us. Yes, it's in the often-not-seen pages of the Old Testament and was written many years ago, but it's relevant for today. It illustrates what we should do when confronting a crisis.

Let's recap what Jehoshaphat and the people of Judah did:

- Resolved to inquire of the Lord
- Rehearsed God's track record
- Admitted they had no power on their own
- Fixed their eyes on God

- Listened to God and took to heart the message he gave them
- Worshiped and praised God

And here's what God did: he set ambushes and defeated the enemy, gave the people reason to rejoice, caused other kingdoms to fear him, and (according to verse 30) Jehoshaphat's kingdom was at peace because God had given him rest on every side.

God will do the same for us if we execute his battle plan and follow his advice.

Oh God, how I love you! You are a big God for whom nothing is impossible. Thank you for your encouraging words and for your promise. I don't have to be afraid. I don't have to be discouraged. I don't have to fight the battle, because it's yours. You will give me deliverance, and you will be with me. I can count on that when I look to you for my help. Thank you, Lord, for giving me a fight song—praise. It's an easy song to sing because you're so praiseworthy. I praise you for who you are. I praise you for what you can do. I praise you for being my victorious God.

POWER STATEMENT

I will sing my fight song daily.

REFLECTION AND RESPONSE

If praise is our fight song, take time to rehearse it. Praise God for who he is and how big he is. Write out your praises to him.

40

Determine to Trust God Even If

When I am afraid, I will put my trust and faith in You.
Psalm 56:3 AMP

Have you ever been in a spot where you were forced to make an excruciating decision, and you weren't sure what to do? And whatever decision you made could have dire consequences? Chances are pretty good that if you haven't already faced this dilemma, you will sometime in the future.

How do you handle it? Where do you find courage when there's no courage to be had?

I've never known such great fear as the few times I had to intervene in a life-and-death situation. On each of the occasions, I needed to act quickly. I didn't have a day or hours or even minutes to mull things over, nor did I have the luxury of anyone's wise counsel. What I really wanted to do was curl up in a fetal position, hide under the covers on my bed, weep and wail uncontrollably, and ask why someone else couldn't fill my shoes. But my only recourse was to cry out to God, do what I thought was right, and take the next step in spite of my great fear. I had to trust God even if …

I'm reminded of two accounts in the Bible when people were put in unthinkable positions. The first is Queen Esther's predicament. If she approached the king in the inner court without being summoned, which was against the law, she could be put to death. Yet if she didn't take the risk, all of the Jewish people, including her, would be annihilated. Esther requested that every Jew in the area fast and pray for three days. She said, "After that I'll go to the king, and even if I perish, I perish." (Her story is found in the Old Testament book of Esther.)

The second is the crisis Shadrach, Meshach, and Abednego faced. They could either compromise their faith and bow down in worship to a golden image, or be thrown immediately into a blazing furnace. (See Daniel 3 for the rest of the story.) When told that they refused to bow to the idol, a furious King Nebuchadnezzar asked the young men who would rescue them from his hand if they were thrown into the furnace. They answered with, "The God we serve is able. He will rescue us from your hand. But even if he doesn't, we will not serve your gods or worship the golden image."

Life is full of extreme scenarios. Although not all of them are as drastic as those mentioned above, we still must determine in our own minds whether we will trust God even if the outcome isn't easy.

God doesn't guarantee that we will escape pain and hardship. But he does promise that he will be with us, he's proven that his grace is sufficient, and he's shown again and again that he can bring about good from bad.

Making the decision to trust God "even if" is the most courageous thing we can do. Do you have what it takes to trust him?

Oh God, I don't like thinking about these scenarios because they make me uncomfortable. I don't like the tough stuff. But I have no guarantees that I won't be faced with something similar in the future. I need to grapple with a hard question. Am I willing to trust you even if …? Lord, I know trusting you comes from relationship and experience. Would you help me to know you better? Would you help me to keep my eyes open to see you at work? Would you help me remember that you are able and that you can rescue? Would you remind me that your grace is sufficient? May I please you with how I answer the "even if …" question.

POWER STATEMENT

Because I know who God is and how big God is, I can trust him even if …

REFLECTION AND RESPONSE

Think about the "even if …" question. Will you make the hard decision? Will you stand up for your convictions? Will you put your life on the line? Will you trust God even if …? Grapple with that for a while.

Power
Statements

1. I have the power to be still. Rather than dwelling on my circumstances and letting them overwhelm me, I will fix my thoughts on God.

2. Because I know God, I can cease striving for control. I trust him to take care of my needs.

3. I AM WHO I AM is a present-tense God. I have no reason to worry or fear because he is with me right now.

4. I will set the Lord always before me. I am unshakable when he is at my right hand.

5. Rather than trying to understand everything, I will trust God with all my heart, and I will acknowledge him in all my ways. When I do that, he will make my paths straight.

6. I have no worries because my heavenly Father knows my needs.

7. Almighty God is my refuge and fortress. I can find rest in his warm embrace.

8. I can trust God today and tomorrow because he has shown me his ability in the past.

9. When I sit in the quiet with God, I find rest for my soul.

10. I will thank God in spite of my circumstances because thanksgiving puts my focus on him and leads to peace.

1. God has given me an extraordinary gift that came at an exorbitant price. How can I not be grateful?

2. I will consistently thank God because God consistently gives. Daily I will count and appreciate his many blessings.

3. I will gratefully acknowledge God's goodness in my life, even in the midst of trials and afflictions. My needs will never exceed his provision.

4. To show my gratitude for God's kindness and goodness, I will brag on him whenever I can, serve him faithfully and with excellence, share the gifts he's given me with others, and love others as he's loved me.

5. Because God has extended his grace to me, I will gratefully extend grace to others.

6. When I'm thankful in all circumstances, my life changes for the better.

7. I realize how blessed I am when I open my eyes to all I have.

8. I will engage the WOW factor and enjoy God's artistry. I will acknowledge God's power and give him praise.

9. With God there is never lack. The more intentionally aware I am, the more bounteous his blessings become.

10. I will praise the Lord at all times. I will constantly speak his praises. I will tell of the Lord's greatness, and I will encourage others to do the same.

THE POWER TO BE STRONG

1. I am strong. I know who I am, and I realize my value comes from God.

2. When confronted with negative messages, I will contradict them with truth. I will not allow them to chip away at my strength.

3. I am incomparable. God gave me my own ordained days to do things nobody else can do.

4. I will be strong in the Lord and in his mighty power. I have all I need to defeat the enemy and to remind him what a loser he is.

5. Because I trust in the Lord and have made him my hope and confidence, I will be strong and productive, like a tree with deep roots.

6. I will rejoice in problems and trials because they help me develop endurance, strength of character, and confidence.

7. Joy is possible in all circumstances. I will find joy in God, and it will be on full display.

8. When I wait for God and keep my attention on him, I gain spiritual muscle and learn valuable truths.

9. I want God to remain the strength of my heart; therefore, I will store up spiritual resources today.

10. God keeps me strong through the help of others. I will gratefully accept their support.

1. I will live like I believe God is who he says he is and will do what he says he will do.

2. When God asks me to do something, I will say yes, even if it's scary. Who I am doesn't matter. Who God is, does.

3. I will remember that God is a promise keeper, and I'll cling to his promises regardless of how things appear.

4. Because God is with me, I can be strong and courageous. I have no reason to be afraid.

5. I have the unmatched power of the living God at work on my behalf. I will look beyond the size of my giants and see the size of my God.

6. When I trust and obey, then get out of the way, God will show up and show off.

7. God will lead me on unknown roads and guide me on unfamiliar paths. I can trust him to turn my darkness to light and make the rough places smooth.

8. When circumstances are beyond my control and I don't know what to do, I will resolve to inquire of the Lord.

9. I will sing my fight song daily.

10. Because I know who God is and how big God is, I can trust him even if …

About the Author

To some she's known as Twila Belk, but to others she's known as the Gotta Tell Somebody Gal. She loves to talk, especially about her Lord—Almighty God. Whether she's writing, speaking, or teaching, Twila's desire is to offer hope and encouragement for people to get their eyes fixed on him.

As a Christian communicator, Twila's goal is making important truths easy to understand. She enjoys laughing and promoting laughter, but even more than that, she's passionate about helping her audiences discover who God is and how big God is and proving that he can be trusted. She has lots and lots of proof of God's faithfulness and goodness, and she just has to tell somebody!

The Power to Be is Twila's seventh book, and she's contributed to several others. Her last title, a one-year devotional also published with BroadStreet, is *Raindrops from Heaven: Gentle Reminders of God's Power, Presence, and Purpose*. She's had the pleasure of speaking at retreats, banquets, outreach events, church services, women's conferences, Women's Connection, Women's Aglow, MOPS, schools, baby showers, bridal showers, Christmas parties, Victorian teas, mother/daughter events, and even a wedding reception!

In addition to writing and speaking, Twila enjoys teaching and keynoting at writers conferences across the nation. Her mission is to do whatever she can to make God famous. That includes being a champion for others who have a message of hope and encouragement—one that points people to God.

Twila and her husband, Steve, live in Bettendorf, Iowa, not far from the Mississippi River and the home of *American Pickers*, John Deere tractors, and Whitey's ice cream. She is Mom to three grown children and Grandma to three precious little boys.

For more information, visit
www.gottatellsomebody.com.